The
Children's
Bible

Anne de Vries

The
Children's
Bible

Anne de Vries

CHRISTIAN FOCUS

© Text Anne de Vries
© 1996 Illustrations & information boxes
Christian Focus Publications Ltd.

ISBN 1-85792-166-6

This edition published in 1996 by
Christian Focus Publications Ltd
Geanies House, Tain, Ross-shire,
IV20 1TW, Scotland, UK.

Reprinted in 1997, 1999, 2000

Contents

THE OLD TESTAMENT

THE NEW TESTAMENT

184,   234,
185,   236,
189,   238,
190,   341,
192,   244,
195,   246
197, 249,
198,
201,
204,
205,
306,
308,
310,
313,
314,
316,
220,
224,
225,
228,
229,
332,
334,

Book Mark

9,	76,	135,
10,	78,	138,
12,	82,	141,
14,	83,	142,
17,	85,	144,
22,	88,	147,
25,	90,	150,
30,	93,	152,
33,	96,	153,
35,	99,	156,
38,	102,	157,
40,	104,	160,
42,	107,	161,
45,	108,	164,
49,	110,	167,
51,	112,	168
56,	114,	169
57,	119,	172
60,	133,	173
63,	124,	175,
66,	125,	176
70,	128,	178
74,	131,	180

THE OLD
TESTAMENT

Why the week has seven days

In the beginning God made heaven and earth. In heaven everything was beautiful, bright and happy. God lived there with the angels but nobody lived on the earth. It was cold, dark and very still and the whole world was covered with water. Then God thought he would make the earth a place where all sorts of plants and animals could live.

He said, 'Let there be light,' and light appeared because everything that God commands happens. When evening came, it grew dark again and God said, 'Let us call the light, day, and the darkness, night.' That was how the first day was born and how it ended with the coming of the first night.

On the second day, God went on with his work to make the world. He said, 'Now let there be a blue sky above the earth!' No sooner had he commanded it than the sky was there. Then it was evening again, and the second day was over.

On the third day, God looked at the earth and saw it was still covered with water. He took the water away from parts of the world and made dry places. God said, 'The water will be called the sea, and the dry parts, land.' After that God made all kinds of plants to grow on the land. He made flowers and trees and grass and wheat.

On the fourth day, God made the sun. Early in the morning the sun lay low in the sky, but as the day passed it climbed higher and higher until it made all the earth warm. The flowers turned their heads towards the sun and blossomed in the soft warm light. Then, as evening came, the sun dropped lower and lower until finally it disappeared from sight.

That night, however, it didn't get quite so dark, for God had made the moon too, and high up in the sky were the twinkling stars. God said, 'From now on the sun shall shine in the daytime and the moon shall shine at night.'

On the fifth day God made the fish in the sea and the birds in the air. He made big fish and little fish. He made them graceful, and their scales would shine with many colours under the water.

God gave the birds magnificent feathers with all the hues of the rainbow and he gave them voices so that they could sing their songs as they flew among the trees. He taught the birds how to build their nests where they would lay their eggs from which baby birds would come. At last the fifth day was over.

The sixth day was a wonderful day. First God made all the animals, like horses, cows, rabbits and sheep. He made cats, dogs, elephants and mice - all the living things, both male and female.

Then God said, 'Let us make man.' So God made the first man and called him Adam. God said, 'Adam, you will look after all the things I have made. You will rule over the fish, the birds and all the animals. All of them must obey you but you must obey me!' Adam listened carefully and understood.

The sixth day came and passed and on the seventh day God rested from his work, for in six days he had made everything.

dam & Eve

The Lord God took very good care of Adam, as a mother and father would care for their child, for he wanted Adam to be completely happy. He made a lovely garden for Adam to live in, where the flowers always bloomed and the birds sang in the trees. God made the garden with fruit on the trees. It was the most magnificent place in all the world, where nothing was ugly. The garden was a wonderful place where Adam could remain happy for ever. It was called the Garden of Eden.

Sometimes God would come to Adam to talk to him when he was walking in the garden. When Adam heard God's voice he was very happy to have God so close to him. Adam took care of the garden and ate as much as he pleased of the things that grew there.

But there was one tree from which he was not allowed to eat. That tree stood in the middle of the garden and it was called the tree of the knowledge of good and evil. God had told Adam: 'You may eat as much as you like from any of the trees, but not from this one. If you eat the fruit from this tree you will die!' Adam

listened very carefully to God's instructions and whenever he came to the tree he did not eat the fruit.

One day God brought all the animals to Adam. He asked Adam to give each of them a name and the names he gave them would remain theirs for ever. But Adam felt very lonely as there were no other human beings to keep him company. The Lord knew exactly what Adam was thinking, for he had waited for this very moment. Of course, God knows everything and Adam didn't have to speak to be understood. God said, 'It is not good for Adam to be alone.'

Then God put Adam to sleep and when he woke there was a woman with him. God had made her for him, to be his wife and friend. Her name was Eve. Adam was very happy for he would no longer be alone. He took Eve with him through the garden and showed her everything. He was careful to point out the tree in the middle of the garden and explained why they must not touch the fruit. Adam and Eve were very happy. They had no pain, were never sick and knew no sadness nor fear, for they lived close to God. God was their father and they were his children.

The Snake, the Fruit and the First Sin

One day all this changed, and it was Adam and Eve's fault. Eve was walking in the garden when she found herself close to the forbidden tree. As she approached the tree she heard a voice she had never heard before. It wasn't Adam and it certainly wasn't God. Eve stopped walking and stood very still. She looked and listened and saw that it was a snake that was speaking to her. It stared at her with its small beady eyes and said: 'Listen to me, is it true that you may not eat of any tree in the garden? Did God tell you that?'

Eve answered, 'Yes, we may eat of all the trees, except this one. God told us that if we eat the fruit of this tree, we shall die.'

Then the sly snake whispered, 'No, you will not die. God said you would, but it isn't true. If you eat the fruit from this tree you will be even happier than you are now, and you will be just as wise and strong as God Himself! I know many

things and I know better than God. It's perfectly alright. Go ahead and eat the fruit from this tree!'

Eve looked at the fruit and saw how it shone in the sun. It looked so beautiful, surely it must taste delicious too. Besides, Eve wanted to be as wise as God! Eve reached up to the fruit in the tree and picked a particularly fine-looking one. Part of the fruit she gave to Adam and part she kept for herself. God had clearly warned them not to eat the fruit from this tree, but they ate anyway. They had disobeyed God.

No sooner had they taken the first bite than they knew that the snake had lied to them. They could feel it in their hearts, for they were no longer happy. They felt afraid, sad, and ashamed of themselves, because for the first time they noticed they had no clothes. Quickly they picked some large leaves to make something to cover themselves.

Suddenly they heard the voice of God! The voice, which had always made them so happy before, made them terribly afraid now and they ran quickly to hide in the bushes. They hoped that God would not find them.

God knows everything so of course he found them. He called to Adam, 'Adam, where are you?' Adam and Eve trembled as they came out from behind the bushes. They were so ashamed that they didn't dare to look at God. 'Did you eat the fruit from that tree?' he asked. His voice sounded both angry and sad.

'Yes, Lord, but Eve gave it to me.' Adam answered. And Eve added in a frightened whisper, 'Yes, Lord, but the snake told me that I should go ahead and eat the fruit.'

God was angry with the snake but was angrier with the enemy who had told the snake what to say. He was the one who was really to blame! The enemy's name was Satan. He was jealous of God and wanted to spoil his wonderful world. This is exactly what he succeeded in doing, for Adam and Eve could no longer be friends with God. They had disobeyed him and could never again speak with him in the beautiful Garden of Eden. Having eaten the forbidden fruit, they had to leave the Garden.

But God still loved his two disobedient children dearly. He loved them so much, he promised everything would one day be well again between God and mankind. He told Eve she would have children, and that some day a baby would be born who would defeat Satan. (God was talking about the Lord Jesus who would be born many years later in Bethlehem.)

He took animal skins and made clothes so that Adam and Eve would not shiver with the cold when he sent them away from the Garden of Eden. To make sure they could never come back again he sent an angel to stand guard at the gate.

ain & Abel

God no longer allowed Adam and Eve to live in the Garden of Eden. Their life had been very happy there but now it was sad and difficult. But it was all their own fault because they had disobeyed God.

One day something happened which made them happy. Adam and Eve had a little baby boy. They called the baby Cain. Later another child was born who was called Abel.

The two little boys grew fast, and soon they learned to walk and talk. Adam and Eve taught them about the Lord God. They told them that they must love God and always obey him.

As the years passed Cain and Abel grew up and they had to work hard like

their father.   Cain became a farmer and Abel became a shepherd. Cain and Abel knew that all things came from God. They also knew how to thank the Lord and to give him something in return for his loving care.

When Abel wanted to bring an offering to the Lord he would pick out the best sheep he had in the flock. This he would call 'God's sheep'. He would then gather dry branches and sticks which would burn easily. First he would pile stones together, on top of which he would put all the dry branches he had collected. Then he would kill the sheep he had chosen and place it carefully on top of the sticks Abel would then put hot coals under the branches and as soon as the wind caught the flames, the sticks would begin to burn. Because the fire was very hot, the sheep would burn too and the smoke would rise to heaven.

Then Abel would kneel and say with great reverence, 'Dear Lord, I love you very much. I want to give you this offering to show you how thankful I am.' The Lord always hears when people pray, and when he heard Abel, he knew that he really loved him and he was happy to receive his offering.

But Cain did not love the Lord. He also brought offerings to God. First he made a pile of stones, on which he put dry branches. Then he stacked some of his wheat on the sticks and set fire to it. Cain also prayed, but he wasn't really thankful. He thought, 'Why do I have to thank the Lord? Didn't I plant the wheat myself and didn't I work hard to make it grow?' God saw what was in Cain's heart and he knew that Cain didn't really love him. Because of this, the Lord did not like Cain's offering.

Cain became angry with God and his brother Abel. He became jealous because God always favoured Abel. He couldn't understand why the Lord made Abel happy but not him. Cain couldn't get this out of his mind and the more he thought about it the angrier he became with Abel. He began to hate his brother and was cruel to him.

God warned Cain. 'Cain, why are you so angry and jealous? Isn't it your own fault? If you love me, I will make you happy too, but if you do not love me how can you be happy?' But Cain did not listen and went on doing as he wanted.

One day he said to his brother, 'Let's go to the field.' When they were alone there Cain began to fight with Abel. He hit Abel so hard that he killed him.

When Cain saw what he had done he was very afraid. He hoped nobody had seen what he had done and he ran away. But God had seen it! The Lord called out to Cain and asked, 'Where is your brother Abel?'

Cain lied and talked back to God. 'I don't know! I don't have to take care of my brother, do I?'

God said, 'Because you have done this, I will not allow your wheat to grow on your fields. You must go away, for you may no longer live here. From now on I will have nothing to do with you. No matter where or how far you go, you will never again find rest. Nor will you ever be happy again!'

That is just what happened. Cain went far away from home but he kept thinking about his brother Abel whom he had beaten to death, and was unhappy and afraid for the rest of his life.

Adam and Eve had lost both their sons in one day. When they went out to look for their boys they found Abel lying on the ground. Adam and Eve buried their dead son in the ground. They were very sad but after a while the Lord made them happy again when they had many more sons and daughters. One of their boys looked very much like Abel and he too loved the Lord. Adam and Eve named him Seth.

oah

This is the story of a man called Noah who built a wonderful boat. It was very large - over a hundred and forty metres long - and took a long time to build. Noah and his three sons, who were called Shem, Ham and Japheth, built it together out of wood. They cut down tall trees, from which they cut beams and planks. Though there was lots of room for many people, only Noah, his wife, his sons and their wives planned to go on the ship.

Sometimes, when the four men were working, other people would come to have a look at the big ship. When they saw it, they would laugh and make fun of Noah and his three sons.

'You can't sail with that ship,' they shouted. 'Can't you see it's standing on dry ground? How can you move such a huge boat to the water?'

'The water will come here!' said Noah. 'There will be water everywhere, over the entire earth. God has said so. He will punish people because they have become so wicked and will no longer obey him. Everyone who isn't in the ark when the water comes will drown!' When the people heard this they laughed even louder.

'Don't laugh', said Noah, 'Listen and ask God to forgive you for your disobedience; then you too may come into the ark.'

The people thought this was very funny indeed. They laughed and laughed and laughed. They shouted, 'We're not going to pray to God! Let the water come, we're not afraid!'

The people on the earth had become very bad and didn't seem afraid of punishment. They behaved as though they could do whatever they wanted. In fact, they acted as though there was no God at all. The Lord had often warned them, but they didn't care. He had been very patient with them and because they wouldn't listen to him, they would be punished. This is why God had told Noah to build the ark. Noah loved the Lord and neither he nor his wife and children would be punished.

God told Noah exactly how he was to build the ark. There was to be a door here, a window there, and inside there were to be many little rooms. There was

to be a good roof over the entire ark, and all the cracks between the planks were to be filled with thick tar so that no water could seep in.

For a long time the people could hear hammering and sawing from early morning until late at night. The people laughed and joked about the boat, and wouldn't listen to Noah's warning of the great flood that was to come.

One day the hammering stopped and the saws were silent. The huge ark was ready. Then God told Noah that he had to put animals, male and female, two by two, into the ark. They all went into the ark, big and small, each into pens where there was food waiting for them.

The people saw all this and wondered what was happening, but they still wouldn't listen until it was too late. Noah and his family went into the ark and the door was closed. For a week the ark stood waiting, and then... the rains came.

First the sun disappeared as heavy clouds drifted across the sky. It became as dark as night and then it began to rain. Never before had it rained so much. It poured, splashed and streamed down to the ground without stopping.

The big ship stood in the darkness as the rain ran off the roof and streamed down the sides. Soon the water round the ark got deeper and deeper until it floated. Then the wind pushed it along and it began to sail. But where was it going? Noah and the other people in the boat didn't know, but the Lord knew and he steered the boat across the water. It continued to rain and the water rose higher and higher on the earth. First of all, houses disappeared, then the trees, until finally even the highest mountains were covered. The only life left was in Noah's ark, apart from the fish in the sea. Everything else had drowned.

God drove the dark clouds away and it stopped raining. Once again the sun began to shine. Nowhere was the earth to be seen. There was only a big deep sea. The eight people on the ark were not afraid because they knew that God would take good care of them. Some day they would all live on the earth again.

For a long time the ark sailed on. Then, without warning, it hit something with a bang and could go no further. It had come to rest on a high mountain and there it was to stay until the earth was dry again. The water was slowly going down, and soon Noah could see the tops of other mountains. Noah could hardly stand the long wait; it took such a long time for the water to go down.

One day he went to the room in which the birds were roosting, took a big black raven to the window, and set it free. The raven which Noah set free was very happy to be out of the ark and didn't return at the end of the day. Already there was enough food on the water for it to live.

Then Noah let a dove out of the ark. All day long the dove flew back and forth looking for little seeds to eat. But there weren't any seeds to be found and when evening came the dove was very tired and flew back to the ship. It was too soon for the dove to be able to live on the earth. When Noah saw the dove he put his hand out of the window and brought it back into the ark.

Noah waited for a week before he

sent the dove out again. Once more it returned to the boat but this time it brought something with it. The dove brought back a leaf from a tree! It seemed to Noah as though the dove was trying to tell him, 'Look, Noah, it won't be long now, the trees are already out of the water.'

Noah waited for another week and when he freed the dove for the third time it did not come back. It had found food and could now live on the earth too. Then Noah opened the door of the ark and waited for God to speak. Finally, the Lord said, 'Now you may leave the ark with your wife and children and all the animals.'

Noah brought an offering to the Lord. When the smoke rose to heaven, Noah and his family knelt down and thanked God for caring for them during the flood. God saw the offering and saw how pleased and thankful they were. The Lord promised that he would never again send such a great flood to the earth. He said, 'When it rains you do not have to be afraid that I will destroy the whole world. If you look up you will sometimes see my rainbow in the sky. I will also see it and it will be a sign that the world will never again be drowned with a flood.

HOW BIG WAS THE ARK?

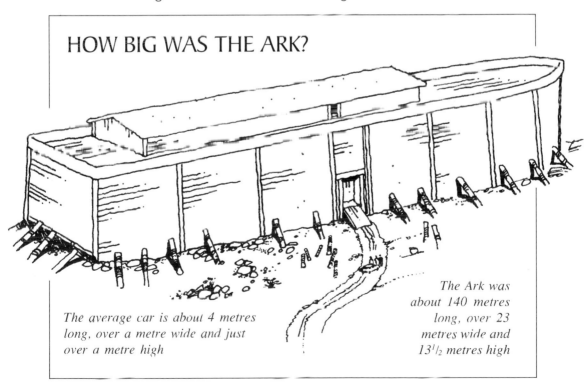

The average car is about 4 metres long, over a metre wide and just over a metre high

The Ark was about 140 metres long, over 23 metres wide and 13¹/₂ metres high

braham

Once there was a very rich man called Abraham. He had many sheep, cattle, donkeys and camels. Abraham had a wife called Sarah. God told him that he had to set off on a long journey with his wife, his relatives, his servants and all his animals.

God said, 'Abraham, you have to move to another country. Don't be afraid, for I will show you where it is. I will help the people who are good to you and will punish those who harm you. Your children will live in this new country.' Abraham loved God and when he heard Him speaking he did what he was asked to do.

It was a long tiring journey. Abraham rode ahead of the others on one of the camels. Beside him rode his nephew Lot, who was very eager to go to that distant country along with his uncle Abraham. Behind the two men rode Sarah with Lot's wife, and behind them followed the sheep with their lambs, the cows with their calves, and all the other animals with their little ones. There were also the servants who had to keep the animals together. They went along high mountains and through thick woods. They rode through deserts where there was nothing but sand. They passed through many countries which Abraham had never visited before.

Each evening they would stop and pitch their tents for the families. The animals, of course, had to stay outdoors, where they huddled close together and slept, guarded by the servants. Each morning everybody would get up and travel on. Abraham wasn't at all afraid on the long trip because he knew the Lord was showing him the way.

One day Abraham came to a big river. They had to cross it but there was no bridge or boat to let them go over. Abraham looked and found a place where the water was shallow and he rode across. All the animals and all the people followed behind. When they reached the other side they were in the country the Lord had promised them. The name of the country was Canaan.

The Lord said, 'Abraham, I will give this land to your children and your children's children.' But there was a problem, for Abraham and Sarah had no children.

Although Abraham and Sarah were no longer young, they didn't doubt what God had told them. Abraham thought, 'It must be true, if God has said it! How this will happen I don't know, but the Lord knows. Whatever God says I believe always happens.' Abraham brought an offering to the Lord to show him how happy and thankful he was. Then he waited patiently for the time when God would give him and Sarah a baby.

Abraham and his nephew Lot lived happily in that new country, but after a while they realised that they could no longer stay together. Abraham had many sheep and so had Lot. There were hundreds of animals. Each year more young animals were born and the number of the herds kept increasing. Finally the time came when there was no longer enough grass for all of the animals. Lot's servants became angry with the servants of Abraham.

'Go away!' they said. 'This grass is for our sheep!'

'Oh no', replied Abraham's servants, 'this grass is ours!'

Every day there were fresh quarrels and the situation grew worse and worse. Soon Abraham knew that they would have to separate. He took Lot to a high mountain from where they could look out over the whole country. Abraham said, 'Lot, it isn't right that our servants quarrel like this. We had better not stay together. You choose where you want to live. If you choose the country towards the right, I will go towards the left. Or, if you prefer the country to the left, I will go to the right.'

When Lot looked, he saw an area where everything looked lush and green. His eyes shone when he saw that lovely land. There was room for many more animals and there was plenty of grass. Lot could get even richer there than he already was.

In the land which Lot had seen were also two cities. They

were called Sodom and Gomorrah and the people who lived there were wicked and godless. Lot didn't mind this so much because he could get very rich and that was all he cared about. Lot chose this beautiful land and he moved close to the city of Sodom.

Lot had chosen the best land it seemed, but the Lord said to Abraham, 'Don't be sad, Abraham, for later on I will give this entire country to your children. Do you know how many children I will give you? Do you know how many people will live here in the years to come? As many as there are grains of sand on the seashore!'

Many years passed but still Abraham and Sarah had no child from God. At last Sarah said with great sadness, 'Look how old we are; we will probably never have a child now.' Abraham replied, 'Oh yes, we will have a son as God has promised.' But in his heart Abraham was sad at times because it took so long for God to give them the promised child.

One night, God spoke to Abraham and said, 'Don't be sad, Abraham, am I not caring for you?'

Abraham said, 'Oh yes, Lord, but we still have no baby!'

A braham & Lot

Then the Lord took Abraham outside and said again, 'Look up towards the sky and count all the stars you can see.' Abraham couldn't do this, of course, because there were far too many stars twinkling in the night.

Then the Lord said, 'Listen, Abraham - for I shall give you as many children as you see stars in the sky. This is how great a nation it will be. I will watch over the people for they will be the people of God.'

When Abraham heard this he was happy again, for he believed what the Lord had told him. Knowing these things he could wait longer.

Later, whenever Abraham became sad again, he would look up at the stars and say, 'My child will surely come, for God has promised it. And when that child grows up, he too will have children of his own and more children will be born, until there will be as many people as there are stars in the sky.'

Abraham and Lot no longer lived in the same place. While Abraham lived in a tent in the land of Canaan, Lot went to live in a house in the city of Sodom. One day they both received a message from God. For Abraham it was good news, but for Lot it was very bad. It was a very hot summer day but beneath the tree where Abraham had pitched his tent it was nice and cool. From a distance came three men. Abraham didn't know them but as they walked towards his home he got up to greet them. When he came close to them, he asked very politely, 'Won't you come into my tent and rest a while. Perhaps you would like something to eat and drink?'

Abraham led them to a resting place in the shade, the best he could find. He gave them some delicious meat and fresh bread and brought them cold water to drink. Although he didn't know who his guests were he took very good care of them. Suddenly, one of the men asked Abraham, 'Where is Sarah, your wife?'

'Over there, in that tent,' replied Abraham, pointing in the direction of her tent.

'Well,' said the visitor, 'a year from now I shall return and at that time Sarah will have a son.'

When Abraham heard this he was very happy. Now he knew who was sitting with him in the shade of the tree. It was the Lord Himself! To think that the Lord Himself, with two of his angels, had come to tell him this wonderful news! Sarah did not know the man outside her tent was the Lord. She had been listening from inside the tent but she couldn't believe it. 'Look how old I am,' she said to herself and shook her head and laughed.

'Why did Sarah laugh?' asked the Lord, 'Is anything too hard for God?'

Surprised and afraid, Sarah said quickly, 'I did not laugh.' She lied because she was afraid of being punished. The Lord replied, 'You did laugh, yet what I have told you will surely come to pass.'

The three men had to go and Abraham walked part of the way with them. They came to the top of a high hill, from which they could see the cities of Sodom and Gomorrah. The Lord said, 'Abraham, because you are my friend, I am going to tell you something. I am now going to the cities of Sodom and Gomorrah, to see whether the people there still hate God. If they do I must punish them and destroy the two cities!'

Abraham was so surprised he couldn't say a word. Was God really going to destroy the two cities? They certainly deserved it, but Lot lived in Sodom and he wasn't godless. He loved the Lord and perhaps there were others like him.

Abraham fell on his knees before the Lord and humbly asked, 'Lord, maybe there are some people in Sodom who still love you. Maybe there are fifty, Lord.'

The Lord answered, 'If I find fifty who love me, I will pardon the entire city.'

'And what if there are only forty-five, Lord?', Abraham asked. 'I will still save the city,' said God.

'Maybe there are only forty,' said Abraham. 'Then I will still not punish the city,' said God.

'And if there are only thirty, Lord?'

'Even then I will save the city,' replied God.

'Oh Lord, please do not be angry with me, but perhaps there are only twenty people who still love and serve You.'

And the Lord said, 'If I find twenty like that, I will not punish the city.'

Abraham hardly dared to ask again, yet he knew how good the Lord was. Very reverently he asked once more, 'Lord, if there are only ten people who love you, what then?' And he heard the Lord say to him, 'If I find ten people in Sodom who love me, I shall not punish the city, because those ten live there!'

When Abraham dared to look up, he found he was alone. In the distance he saw the men walking towards Sodom. Sadly Abraham walked home. He kept thinking about Sodom but when he reached home he remembered God's wonderful news. The Lord Himself had come to speak to them and Sarah no longer doubted that she would have a child.

Lot received bad news from the two angels who had been with Abraham. Around the city of Sodom was a high wall and in this wall was a gate. There was no other way into the city. It was evening when the two angels reached Sodom. When Lot saw the two strangers coming, he thought, 'I shall take care of those men, for some of the wicked people of Sodom might harm them.' So he took the two men to his house, where he gave them supper and invited them to stay for the night.

Suddenly there was a great noise outside the house! Someone was pounding on the door and there was a great commotion in the street. A voice cried, 'Where are those strangers? We have come to get them; open the door! We'll take care of those strangers for you!' they shouted. The men surrounded the house so that no one could get out and they were shouting angrily. They were such evil men, strangers were not safe in Sodom. Lot, however, was not afraid. He went outside and walked right up to them and said, 'Don't hurt these men! They have done you no harm.' But they just ignored Lot and grew angrier.

'Are you telling us what to do? Come here if you dare, and we'll treat you worse than those strangers.' They almost grabbed Lot but the two angels quickly pulled him inside and locked the door.

Then a miracle happened! The men wanted to break down the door, but no matter how they looked, they couldn't find it! It was as though they had become blind. They looked and looked for the door but it was no-where to be seen. God took care that they wouldn't find it and at last, tired of trying, the men went away. Lot and his house were safe!

Then the angels told Lot why they had come. They were in Sodom to punish the people because of what they had done. They told Lot they were going to destroy the city and all the people in it. It was terrible news!

'But you can be saved, Lot,' said

the angels. 'You must go away with your wife and your two daughters.'

Lot could hardly believe the news. Did he really have to leave? What about his house? Would this be destroyed too? What about all his sheep and cows and his other animals? Must he leave them behind as well? He had worked so hard to get them and had become a rich man. Must he really give up everything? Lot couldn't decide what to do. He didn't want to leave because he loved his house and all his other things.

It was growing lighter outside. The night was over, and the day of punishment for Sodom had come! 'Hurry,' said the angels. 'Come along, otherwise you too will die!' But Lot just sat there. He didn't seem to hear what they were saying. Then the angels took him by the hand and pulled him along. They took his wife and daughters also, through the door and down the street, until they were outside the city. 'Now, run for your lives!' cried the angels, 'Don't stand still, don't even look back, for if you do, you will die.'

Only then did the four of them begin to run. Behind them, the ground began to shake and fire fell from heaven. Houses caught fire and the city was burning.

The ground was torn open and the entire city disappeared into the hole. Everyone in Sodom died that day but Lot and his two daughters were saved. Sadly, however, Lot's wife was so sorry to have to leave her fine house and all her gold that she turned to look back. She was caught in the destruction and died.

Abraham woke up early that morning and climbed the hill to look toward Sodom. A thick cloud of smoke hung over the land; Sodom was no longer there. It was then that Abraham knew that there weren't even ten people in the whole city who loved the Lord.

Lot went with his two daughters to live somewhere in the mountains. He had wanted so much to be rich, but now he lived in a cave like a poor man. He had loved his house and his gold and his animals, but now he had lost everything. He had also loved the Lord but he hadn't lost Him. God was still with him and was Lot's friend.

agar & Ishmael

A year passed and the baby which Abraham and Sarah had been waiting for so long was born. It was a little boy and they called him Isaac. They were very happy, and thankful that this was the child God had promised. He would become the leader of a great people.

Little Isaac grew fast. First he learned to crawl around the tent; then later he learned to walk and talk. The time came for Abraham to give a party for young Isaac who had grown up to be such a big boy.

At the party something happened to spoil the fun. It wasn't Isaac's fault: it was that of another boy called Ishmael, who also lived with them along with his mother Hagar, one of Abraham and Sarah's servants. Ishmael was much bigger than Isaac and he wasn't very kind to the little boy. Ishmael was jealous and he sometimes thought, 'I wish Isaac had never been born. Some day he will be master here and will have almost everything. He is the promised child, but I will have very little.'

At the party Ishmael teased Isaac. He laughed at him and made fun of him. Sarah saw Ishmael and she said to Abraham, 'You must send that boy away and his mother, too. Ishmael can't stay here with Isaac for he always wants to be the leader and he is very mean to Isaac.'

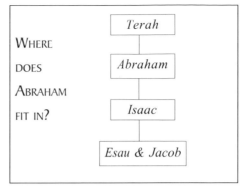

WHERE DOES ABRAHAM FIT IN?

Terah
Abraham
Isaac
Esau & Jacob

DO YOU KNOW?

Although Abraham is an Old Testament character he is also mentioned in the New Testament. You can find him in Acts7:2 and Hebrews 11:8-19. Abraham was known as 'a man of faith'.

Abraham loved Ishmael and Hagar and didn't want to send them away, but eventually Hagar and Ishmael left Abraham's tent. The mother and her son went away, taking with them loaves of bread and a bottle of cold water. Abraham watched sadly as they walked away from the tent door.

Hagar and Ishmael had to walk a long way, for they were going back to the land from which she came before she worked for Abraham. Hagar was thinking of her troubles and her poor little boy and didn't watch where she was going. Soon they were lost in the desert. The sun beat down on them and the sand was very hot. As far as the eye could see there was nothing but sand. Not one tree could they find to give them shade.

Further and further they wandered. Every once in a while they would stop and drink a little water from the bottle. It was so hot they grew very thirsty. No longer did they have a house to live in, nor a bed to rest in. They had no one to take care of them. But God saw them and he would look after them.

Ishmael was terribly thirsty from the heat and very tired from walking on the hot sand. Hagar gave him another drink of water but there wasn't much left, for they had been drinking from it on the way. The bottle was almost empty. Ishmael could hardly walk another step. 'Please mother, I'm so thirsty!' Hagar gave him the bottle and he put it to his lips but it was empty! 'There's no more water!' he cried.

Hagar was startled. She looked round to see if she could find any water. There was none at all. There was no well, no stream, not even a puddle anywhere. There was nobody she could ask for water. There was nothing but hot dry sand around them.

Ishmael was so thirsty that he could walk no further and fell down. He lay on the sand, groaning with pain. Hagar didn't know what to do to help her poor child. She picked him up and took him over to a small bush which she hoped would give him a little shade. There was nothing else she could do.

Ishmael lay there with his eyes closed and his moaning grew softer and softer. Hagar couldn't watch him any longer, for she couldn't bear to see her child die. She walked a little way away, sat down in the sand and cried.

'Oh, my boy,' she sobbed. 'My darling boy, you are dying of thirst, and your mother can't help you!' The tears ran down her cheeks to the burning hot sand.

All at once Hagar looked up. She looked around but saw no one; yet a voice spoke to her, 'Hagar, what is the matter? Don't be afraid. I have heard the boy's cry. Get up and go over to him. I will take care of him.'

Hagar knew this voice well, for it was the voice of God! Now everything would be all right. Quickly she dried her tears and ran to her child. There she saw a well, a deep hole in the ground with sparkling clear water in it. She ran to the well with her water bottle and filled it right to the top. Then she hurried to her boy, held him up and put the bottle to his lips.

Ishmael drank deeply and he opened his eyes. His pale cheeks grew rosy again and, after a while, he was able to get up and walk.

Now they both knew there was somebody who cared for them. Father Abraham wasn't there, but their Father in heaven was and he would always stay close to them. The Lord showed Hagar the way to the country where they would live.

There Ishmael grew into a big strong man. He grew into a good hunter. Every day he hunted in the desert. All his life, he knew that the Lord cared for him.

braham's big test

Isaac had grown up and Abraham loved him more and more every day. Abraham also loved God, for it was God who had given him the child. But whom did Abraham love the most, God or his son Isaac? Abraham often brought offerings to the Lord, which he gave with great reverence and adoration. He would be willing to give God everything he had.

One day God thought, 'I wonder if Abraham loves me more than his son? I want to see if he loves me above all else.' That night God spoke to Abraham: 'You must give your child to me. You must offer him to me on Mount Moriah.'

Abraham was shocked! How could God ask him to sacrifice the son that God had given him and whom he loved so dearly? Did he now have to give him back to the Lord? And hadn't God said that Isaac would live in this land and become the father of a great nation? Abraham didn't understand it but God had said it, and Abraham had to obey and have faith that all would turn out well in the end.

The next morning Abraham got up very early, saddled a donkey, and called two of his servants before going to the tent where Isaac slept.

'Wake up, my boy, we're going on a long journey.' But he didn't tell him what was going to happen.

This sounded wonderful to Isaac. It was probably the most exciting trip Isaac had ever had in his life. It took three days to reach the mountain. However, for Abraham it was the saddest journey he had ever made.

Abraham told his servants, 'You wait here with the donkey. Isaac and I are going a little further. When we have made the offering we will return.'

He really meant it too, because he believed that the Lord would make everything right. Isaac carried the wood, while Abraham carried a pot with burning coals in it. As the two were going up the mountain, Isaac stopped and asked, 'Father, you have the fire and I'm carrying the wood, but where is the lamb we will offer to God?'

Abraham replied, 'The Lord will provide a lamb, my son.' So the two went on together.

When they reached the top of the mountain, Abraham built the altar of stones. He placed the wood on it... then Abraham had to explain. He told Isaac he must be the sacrifice. Putting ropes round Isaac, he placed him on the altar.

Just as Abraham raised the knife a voice said, 'Abraham! Abraham!' God had seen how willingly Abraham would give everything he had. Abraham replied gladly, 'Here I am!'

Then the Lord said, 'Stop, don't hurt the boy! Now I know you love me above all else. You are even willing to give me your only child!'

Abraham cut the ropes from Isaac and, taking him in his arms, he held him tight. Suddenly a rustling noise came from behind him and he saw a ram caught by its horns in the bushes. God had provided a sacrifice! Abraham put the animal on the wood and gave the Lord an offering. Then they went home together. God had made everything work out well in the end. Isaac would become the father of a great people.

J acob & Esau

Isaac became a great man. He lived in the tent of his father, Abraham, and he was the master over everything. Both Abraham and Sarah had died. Isaac didn't live in his father's tent alone. He had a wife whose name was Rebecca and they had two children, Jacob and Esau.

Jacob and Esau were twins, but Esau was just a little bit older as he was born first. Although they were twins they did not look at all alike. Esau's skin was hairy. Jacob's skin was smooth and fair.

Esau was a rough boy, full of life. When he grew a little older, it was hard for him to stay at home for any length of time. He often went far into the fields and woods, where he hunted deer and other wild animals.

Jacob was quieter, and was content to stay in the tent with his mother, or care for the sheep. Jacob loved God and wanted to be his child.

Esau didn't think very often about God, yet Isaac loved Esau more than he loved Jacob. Esau often brought home good meat from his hunting trips. He would cook it just the way Isaac liked it. On the other hand, Rebecca loved Jacob more than his brother. He would stay at home with her and talk with her like a grown man. But which of the two would later live in Isaac's tent, take care of the sheep, goats and other animals? Who was to receive from Isaac the special blessing of the eldest son? Remember, Esau was the first born.

However, Isaac and Rebecca knew, because God had told them it was to be Jacob. Rebecca was pleased with this but Isaac thought he knew better than

God. He said, 'Esau is the eldest, and the eldest must take care of my house. The eldest must receive the special blessing.' Rebecca often thought about the blessing and so did Jacob because he knew that Esau was the elder.

One day Jacob was sitting in front of his tent. He had cooked some lentil soup over a fire and the delicious smell was carried out over the fields on the breeze. Esau had been out hunting all day long and he was very tired and hungry. When he smelled the soup his eyes sparkled and he called out to his brother, 'Give me some of that soup you have there!'

Jacob looked at him slyly and replied, 'You may have it, provided you allow me to be called the elder brother so that I can get the special blessing.'

Esau laughed and answered, 'What do I care about such things; of course you may!'

And so Esau got his lentil soup. Jacob went out of his way to seem nice to his brother; he even gave him some bread with it, but really he had not done the right thing.

Many years passed, and Isaac grew old. He became very weak and finally he went completely blind. Each day, as he lay on his bed in the tent,

he wondered, 'Who will be the master over everything after I die? Surely I will die before long; then who will live in my tent? It must be Esau!'

One day he called Esau and said, 'My son, go to the forest and hunt for a deer. Prepare it for me just the way I like it. Then, after I have eaten, I will give you the special blessing.' Esau left for the woods to hunt for a deer. Now, Esau should have said, 'No father, Jacob must have the blessing, for I promised it to him many years ago.' But instead he thought, 'What do I care about the promise to Jacob. I would like to have the blessing for myself.'

Rebecca overheard all this through the tent wall and she ran to Jacob immediately. 'We have to act quickly', she said, 'if you are to have the blessing. We must deceive your father. Run to the flock and bring me two small goats. I will cook them just the way your father likes them; then you must bring them to him. Your father is blind and you must act just like Esau, so that he won't know the difference.'

But Jacob was afraid. 'Father can feel that I'm not Esau,' he said. 'My hands are soft and smooth, while Esau's are rough and hairy.'

Rebecca had the answer to this.

'Just do as I tell you,' she said, 'and I will take care of all these things.'

So Jacob did as he was told. First he killed the two goats and gave them to Rebecca to cook. Then she gave him Esau's best suit to wear, which had the smell of the woods and fields on them. Cutting the skin of the young goats, she fitted them to Jacob's hands and neck and then sent him to his father's tent.

'Father,' he said.

'Who are you, my son?'

'I am Esau, your eldest boy. I have come back from the woods, with the meat you asked for. Sit up and eat what I have prepared for you; then give me your blessing.'

Isaac noticed something wrong. He said, 'Are you really Esau? You have such a strange voice; come here and let me touch you. Let me feel whether or not you really are Esau.'

Jacob knelt down beside the bed so that Isaac could feel his hands. 'The voice is Jacob's, but the hands are Esau's,' said the old man. Softly he asked just once more, 'Are you really Esau?'

'Yes,' lied Jacob, 'I'm really Esau.'

The meat was beside the bed and it smelled delicious. Isaac ate some then Jacob gave him some wine to drink too. Isaac said, 'Kiss me, my son.' When Jacob bent close to his father, Isaac could smell the clothes of Esau. Smelling the woods and fields in the cloth he was sure it was Esau kneeling beside the bed. Reaching over, he placed his hands on Jacob's head. In doing this, he blessed him and told Jacob that one day he would be the master of all the house. He told him he would be the friend of God. Jacob didn't dare look up. He felt awfully guilty, because he had cheated his old father. Nevertheless he had received the blessing, just as God said would happen.

A little while later Esau came home. He had killed the deer his father had asked for and had come to clean and cook it. When it was ready he brought it in to his father's tent. 'Father, here I am,' he called.

Isaac's heart pounded. Suddenly he knew he had been deceived. Esau shook with anger when he heard about the trick his brother had played. He told everyone, 'When my father is gone, I shall kill Jacob. I will kill that liar!'

Rebecca heard this and she called to Jacob, 'You must go away quickly and live with your uncle in a country far away. When Esau is no longer so angry with you, I'll let you know.'

And so Jacob ran away from his family to hide where his brother Esau couldn't find him. Now he was a poor homeless wanderer because he had lied to his father and Esau. Rebecca lost the boy she loved so much and Isaac was sad too as he lay on his bed.

Jacob makes a new life for himself

Jacob went far away from his home. He didn't want to go but he was afraid of his brother after he had tricked him. It was a long journey to the land where his uncle lived and Jacob felt both lonely and sad. He was sorry for having lied to his blind old father. Jacob thought, 'No one cares about me any more. Maybe even God no longer cares, because I have been so bad.' This was the worst thought of all - to think God might be angry with him and no longer be his friend.

Evening came and the sun set. It became quite dark and there was no house where Jacob might sleep. He would have to sleep outdoors under the open sky. He lay down on the ground and rested his head on a stone. As he lay there, looking up at the stars, God was not very far away. Surely God would never again look at Jacob, the deceiver. Jacob thought to himself, 'How I wish the Lord would forgive me. How sorry I am for what I have done; I want so much to be his friend.' Then he fell asleep.

While Jacob slept, he had a strange dream. In the dream he saw a long ladder which reached up to heaven. Angels were walking up and down the ladder. At the very top of the ladder was the Lord God himself. His face was friendly as he looked down on Jacob and he said, 'I am the Lord, the God of Abraham and of Isaac your father. Don't be afraid! Go on your way, for I am going with you and I will also bring you back safely. You may still be my friend. Many years from now your children will live in this very land where you are now sleeping.'

Jacob woke up. He had been dreaming for a long time and it was morning. He remembered the dream.

The Lord had said that he would care for Jacob and so he wanted to mark the spot where he had slept. He used the stone on which he had rested his head as a memorial. He wanted to bring an offering to God to show how thankful he was. He took a small jar of oil that he had with him and poured it on the stone as an offering, praying, 'Lord, thank you for being so good to me. I want to love you always and when I return to this place I will bring another offering.' No longer feeling afraid or lonely he travelled on his way. God went with him and looked after him, bringing him safely to his uncle's home.

Jacob returns

Jacob became the servant of his uncle in the far away land. He took care of his uncle's sheep and his cattle. When he was there he married Leah, one of his uncle's daughters. Later he married another daughter called Rachel, and he had many children.

Jacob stayed with his uncle for a very long time. He worked hard and became a rich man with his own sheep, cattle and other animals. Many years ago, Jacob's mother had said, 'I will let you know when you may come back. I will tell you as soon as Esau is no longer angry with you.' He waited to hear from his mother but she did not get in touch with him.

One day God said, 'Jacob, now you must go back to your own country. I am going with you, so don't be afraid, for I will take care of you.'

Jacob prepared for the long trip. He took his wives and his children, his servants and his maids, his sheep, his cattle and his camels. It was a very long parade of people and animals, just like Abraham's procession to Canaan so many years before. Jacob had fled from Canaan all alone. Now he was returning to his own country a very rich man, with many children and servants and animals that all belonged to him. How well the Lord had taken care of him.

At first his uncle didn't want to let Jacob go to Canaan. But the Lord told him, 'You must let Jacob go.'

It was a long, tiring trip but finally Jacob came close to the land where he had lived as a child with his father and mother. Then he grew afraid when he remembered what had happened so long ago, how angry his brother Esau had been and how he had wanted to kill Jacob. Would Esau remember? Would he still be angry with Jacob? He hoped Esau had forgotten, because Esau was so strong and rough, if he was still angry with Jacob and wanted to fight, surely Jacob would lose!

Jacob thought to himself, 'I know what I'll do. I'll send Esau a message that I want to be friends with him.' So he sent Esau a gift of sheep, goats and camels. It was a very big herd of animals; a few servants went ahead to present them to Esau.

When the servants returned they said, 'Master, be careful! Esau is coming with many strong men. There are as many as four hundred, and all of them have swords and spears with which to fight.' Jacob was very afraid because he thought Esau was coming to punish him by killing them all. He was so terrified he couldn't sleep. Long after all the others were in bed he remained outside in the dark night. Then he remembered God, and God's promise to care for him. Jacob said, 'Dear Lord, help me now, just as you promised you would. I'm very afraid of Esau!' No sooner had Jacob prayed than there was an angel with him. The angel stayed all night and when morning came Jacob was no longer afraid. He knew Esau wouldn't harm him because God was with him.

That very day Esau came. The ground shook as Esau rode towards Jacob with all his servants. Clouds of dust blew up into the air. It seemed very dangerous but Jacob was no longer afraid. Calmly he walked over to Esau; then, to his surprise, Esau put his strong arms around Jacob and kissed him! He wasn't angry at all, but glad that his brother had come back at last.

TWINS

Twins are often very alike but not always. Esau and Jacob were twins, but were very different from each other.

Jacob

He had smooth skin.
He stayed at home around the tents.

Esau

He had red hairy skin.
He was a hunter who enjoyed outdoor life.

The Lord had taken all the anger out of Esau's heart. The two brothers sat down and talked together, for they had a lot to talk about. It was a wonderful day. The children all came over to kiss their uncle Esau. Before evening came, Esau left and Jacob travelled on to the land of Canaan until finally he reached his home. He learned that his mother Rebecca had died since he left home, but that his father Isaac was still living and was very happy that his son had returned. Later, after Isaac died, Jacob went to live in his father's tent.

Joseph

Jacob had many children. One of them was called Joseph. He had ten older brothers and one younger than himself. The little brother's name was Benjamin and his father loved him very much. But Jacob loved Joseph even more than Benjamin. As a matter of fact, he loved Joseph more than all his other sons. Sometimes he spoiled him a little. Once he gave Joseph a beautiful coat with many colours in it: red, blue, purple and gold. It was so magnificent it looked like a prince's coat.

Most of the time little Benjamin stayed at home with his father and his brother Joseph while the other brothers were out in the field looking after the animals. Sometimes Joseph would help his brothers, but it wasn't much fun, as they were always jealous of him because he had received such a beautiful coat from their father. But there were other reasons as well. They were annoyed because whenever the older brothers did anything wrong, Joseph would run home to tell Jacob about it.

One night Joseph had a dream that he was with his brothers in the wheat fields. The wheat had already been cut but it had to be tied up in bundles called sheaves. In his dream Joseph bound a sheaf and laid it on the ground. Suddenly his sheaf stood upright and the sheaves of his brothers formed a ring around it and bowed down to it. Joseph couldn't forget this dream. He told his brothers about it but they got very angry and said, 'You'd really like that, wouldn't you? You'd love us all to bow before you! You'd like to be the ruler over

us! It'll never happen, you silly dreamer!' Then Joseph had another strange dream. He dreamt that the sun, the moon and eleven stars came down from the sky and bowed before him. Even his father scolded him when he told the others about it. Jacob asked him, 'What kind of foolishness is this? Do you really believe we would all bow before you? I, your mother, and all your brothers; how could it ever be?' But Joseph couldn't explain the dream.

Jacob often thought about Joseph's dreams but they made all his brothers very angry. After a while, they became so angry they wanted to kill him. Fortunately, they didn't dare beat him to death as their father was nearby.

One day the brothers took the sheep a long way from home and didn't come back when they were supposed to. Finally Jacob said to Joseph, 'You had better look for your brothers and see if they're alright, I'm worried about them. When you find them come back quickly and tell me how they are.'

So Joseph went out to look for his brothers. When they saw him coming they planned to attack him. 'Look', they said, 'here comes the dreamer, and father isn't here! Now that we have him, we'll kill him, and throw his body into that deep hole over there. We will tell father that a wild animal attacked him. Then we'll see what will come of all those fine dreams!' But the oldest brother said, 'No, let's not do that. Don't kill him! Throw him into the hole alive.'

The oldest brother's name was Reuben. He wasn't quite as bad as the others but he was afraid of them. He thought, if he was clever, he could outsmart them, and save Joseph by returning when it was dark to rescue him out of the horrible pit.

The brothers grabbed Joseph and dragged him away. They tore off his beautiful coat and threw him into the hole. They had absolutely no pity for him and didn't listen when he cried out in fear.

'Just lie there and keep right on dreaming that you're our leader!' Then they sat down close to the pit and ate their lunch, while their younger brother was crying in the hole right next to them.

Reuben, however, wasn't quite so cruel. He took a walk in the field and thought, 'Just wait, Joseph, as soon as it's dark I'll come and help you.' Reuben thought he had fooled his brothers.

It was a good thing for Joseph that there wasn't any water in the old well. He was safe from drowning but he couldn't get out alone because the walls were too steep and slippery. Jacob, of course, was far away and knew nothing about what was going on.

Suddenly Joseph heard voices, and there were his brothers at the mouth of the pit. They had come to pull him out with a rope. But when they pulled him out he noticed that there were strange men with them, and camels with packs on their backs. They looked like traders from another country, and they were giving money to Joseph's brothers.

Suddenly Joseph realised what was happening! His brothers had sold him to the traders. They took Joseph, tied him up and put him on to a camel. He looked back at his brothers and called out, 'Help me, please help me! I want to go home to my father.'

But the brothers paid no attention to him and Reuben wasn't there to help. Later, long after Joseph and the traders were out of sight, Reuben came back, but it was too late. 'Now what?' asked Reuben. 'What will our father say about this?' The other brothers had planned it carefully and knew exactly what to do.

They were wicked and not afraid to make up a false story. First they killed a little goat and poured its blood on Joseph's beautiful coat. Then they took the coat to Jacob saying, 'Look, father, we found this in the field. Isn't this Joseph's coat?' When Jacob saw the coat he thought Joseph had been killed by a wild animal and the poor old man was heartbroken. Jacob said, 'I will never be happy again, now that my dear Joseph is dead!' He didn't know, of course, that the blood on the coat was only goat's blood.

Joseph in Egypt

Jacob really believed that Joseph was dead. But he was very much alive in another country called Egypt where the traders had sold him as a servant to a rich man called Potiphar. Now that Joseph was a slave he could never go home to his father again no matter how much he wanted to. Potiphar had many servants who had to work hard all day long. If one of them was lazy, or if anyone complained, he was punished with a whip.

Joseph was not lazy, nor did he complain. Instead he tried very hard to do his best. He thought, 'God still sees me, even in this far country. God wants me to do the best I can.' Everything went well, for God took good care of Joseph. He blessed him and helped him do his work. Wherever Joseph went things went well, and he turned out to be the best servant in Potiphar's household.

Potiphar noticed this and said to him one day, 'Joseph, you may be the head man over all my servants and over everything I have.' He was free to go anywhere he wished in the house.

Now Potiphar had a wife who was rather sly. One day she tried to trick Joseph into doing wrong. But Joseph said, 'I cannot do that. God sees everything we do. Do you think I would do this sin against God?' So he refused to do what she said. But every time she saw Joseph she spoke to him about it. She wouldn't leave him alone. One day, when Potiphar was away, she grabbed Joseph by his coat and pulled him towards her. 'You must listen to me,' she said. 'You must do as I say!'

Joseph pulled himself free and ran away but he left his coat behind him in her hands. She began to scream and cry, 'Help, help, Joseph attacked me!' Other servants came running and believed her, because they saw Joseph's coat in her hands. When Potiphar came home he listened to his wife's story and he believed her too. He was so angry with Joseph that he had him arrested and thrown into prison along with thieves, murderers and other evil men. He had done nothing wrong, yet he was still being punished.

The Lord saw him there and said, 'Do not be afraid, Joseph, but be patient. I love you and I will take care of you even here in prison.' Joseph wasn't alone. God was still with him, he knew Joseph had done nothing wrong.

Each day the door to Joseph's prison cell opened for just a moment when a man came to bring food. He was the man who was in charge of the prisoners. Day after day he saw Joseph sitting there quietly and patiently. The guard soon realised that there was something different about Joseph. He felt he could trust him. One day he said, 'Come here for a moment, Joseph. You can do something for me. Why don't you help me to take the food to the other prisoners.'

Joseph was glad to be able to do something and again he worked hard to do his best. God blessed him in everything he did, but he remained a prisoner and was not free to leave.

One day two new prisoners were brought in. They were important men from the palace of the king. One was the cup-bearer of the king. He used to pour the king's wine and serve it to him. The other man was the baker for the king. They had both been put in prison because the king was angry with them.

Every morning Joseph gave them their food, but one day when he opened their door, they sat staring and afraid. 'What's the matter?' Joseph asked.

'Oh!' they said. 'We both had a strange dream. We think our dreams mean something but we don't know what.'

'What did you dream about?' asked Joseph.

The cup-bearer described his dream first

'I dreamt that I was out of prison again. I saw a beautiful vine which had three branches. The branches were loaded with big luscious grapes. In my hand I held the golden cup of the king. I pressed the juice out of the grapes and let it run into the cup and then I brought the cup full of good wine to the king.'

While Joseph listened the Lord told him the meaning of the dream. He said, 'The three branches are three days. At the end of three days you will be free and you will again be the cup-bearer of the king.'

Then Joseph asked him, 'Will you ask the king if I may also be set free? I have done no wrong either.'

'Of course!' the cup-bearer promised. He would promise anything if only he could be free again.

Then the baker wanted to tell Joseph his dream.

'I also dreamt I was out of prison again. I walked in the street with three baskets on my head, one on top of the other. In the top basket were delicious cakes for the king, but the birds came and picked at the cakes and ate everything up.'

Joseph looked very sad and said, 'This dream does not bring good news. Those three baskets also mean three days, but in those three days the king will punish you for doing wrong. He will kill you and hang your body from a tree, where the birds will come and pick at your flesh.'

And all these things happened just as Joseph had told them. Three days later the cup-bearer was free and the baker was punished.

But the cup-bearer forgot all about his promise to Joseph. He was so glad to be out of prison he didn't even think about his time there. Joseph waited and waited but no one came to take him out of prison. But God hadn't forgotten him, although he had to stay in prison for another two years before being released. This is how it happened.

Joseph becomes the King's Governor

One night when Joseph was still in prison the king had a strange dream. He dreamt that he was standing near the river, when out of the water came seven fat cattle. They began to eat the grass which grew on the river bank. Then seven more came out of the water but they were skinny.

All at once the thin cattle went over to the fat ones and began to eat them. They ate them all up yet the skinny ones didn't get any fatter. Even though they ate the big fat ones the skinny cattle remained just as thin as before.

The king was so startled he woke up. Realising it was just a dream, he fell asleep again and had another strange dream. This time he saw a tiny wheat plant with seven round ears full of kernels. Another plant began to grow and this also had seven ears, but they were thin and empty, with no kernels in them at all.

The same thing happened as with the cattle. The empty ears bent over the full ears and ate them.

The king woke up again, but this time he couldn't sleep any longer. He called his servants and told them what he had dreamt. 'Surely this means something!' he said. 'Explain it to me.' But none of his servants knew what it meant. With the other servants was the cup-bearer who suddenly remembered Joseph and told the king about him. 'Bring Joseph to me right now,' said the king. Joseph was taken out of prison, washed and given new clothes before being taken to the king. The king asked, 'Can you tell me the meaning of these dreams?'

'No, my king,' Joseph replied. 'Only God knows the meaning of dreams, but perhaps he will tell me.'

Then the king told Joseph what he had dreamt: the dream of the seven fat cattle and seven thin ones; seven ears full of wheat and seven empty ones. Joseph explained, 'These two dreams mean the same thing. First there will be seven very good years. During this time much wheat will grow on the land.

Following this there will be seven bad years, when nothing will grow. The people will then have nothing to eat.'

'Oh,' said the king. 'Then we will die of hunger?'

'No, my king,' replied Joseph. 'You must build warehouses and have the people fill them with wheat. In the seven good years there will be plenty. When the bad years come, you will have food for all the people.'

'Oh good,' shouted the king. 'This will indeed be done. How wise and sensible you are Joseph. You had better take charge of all these matters and of the people of my country. You may do whatever you like. I am the only one over you. I am the king, but you are the governor.'

He took his gold ring and put it on Joseph's finger. He gave him fine clothes to wear and put a gold chain around his neck. Joseph rode in one of the king's coaches through the city. All the people had to bow before Joseph as though he were the king himself.   He was given a beautiful house to live in with many servants and all kinds of attractive things. He had become a very wealthy and important man. But Joseph did not become proud even though he had all these wonderful things. He knew who had really given him all this. Joseph was happy and very thankful.

Joseph's brothers go to Egypt

Everything happened just as Joseph had said. First came the seven good years when a lot of crops grew on the land. There was so much that the people couldn't eat it all, so they brought the surplus to Joseph who arranged for big barns to be built to store the grain.

Then the seven bad years came when nothing would grow on the land. The sun was so hot that all the plants burned and died before they could bear grain. Everywhere in the world people were hungry. Everywhere, that is, except in Egypt, where they had plenty to eat. All the barns were filled to the top. Joseph began to sell grain to those who were hungry and people came from other countries to buy from him.

One day ten men came to Joseph. They had brought many bags along in the hope of buying grain. Joseph couldn't help but stare when he saw who the men were. They were his brothers who had been so cruel to him long ago! Joseph remembered them very well indeed. After all, they had sold him to the traders and shown him no pity at all. Although Joseph knew them immediately they didn't recognise him. They knelt down before him, the dignified governor. Joseph's dream of long ago had come true!

If he had wanted, Joseph could have punished them there and then for the terrible things they had done to him. They were completely at his mercy. He could have had them killed or thrown into prison if he had so wished. But Joseph wasn't angry with his brothers even though they had caused him so much grief. He wanted to forgive them for what they had done and to be kind to them.

He thought to himself, 'Should I tell them that I am Joseph? No, not yet. I want to know if they are still bad. I wonder where Benjamin is?' Putting on a serious face, he said, 'Where did you come from?'

'From the land of Canaan, sir,' they replied. They told him of their old father and a younger brother who had stayed at home. They also told him they were all very hungry. As the governor, Joseph made himself look very angry and said, 'It's all very well for you to tell me these things, but I don't believe you at all. You are lying! You are enemies who have come to spy on this country. I believe a few of you have come to find the shortest way here and later you will come with an army to steal everything we have.'

'No, no sir,' they protested. 'We are honest men who have come to buy grain because we are very hungry!'

Joseph pretended not to believe them. 'I will find out if you are telling the truth. Go home and fetch your youngest brother, then I will believe you. To make sure you will come back one of you must remain here.'

So Simeon remained behind while the others went back home. Joseph had their bags filled and loaded on to the donkeys. Ten donkeys had come from Canaan and ten were going home but one of them went alone, while his master remained behind as a hostage.

The brothers went home feeling sad and afraid. They had got what they wanted but they weren't happy because Simeon had to stay behind in Egypt. Jacob was afraid something awful would happen to Benjamin if he allowed him to go to Egypt so he wouldn't allow them to take him back to the angry governor.

However, as the weeks passed, the supply of grain began to be used up. Finally they had to go back to

Egypt for more, but the brothers didn't dare go there without Benjamin. They knew that the governor would be very angry if they didn't bring the youngest brother and they were afraid for Simeon. It was a desperate situation and finally Judah spoke up and said to Jacob, 'Allow me to take Benjamin, father. I will see no harm is done to him. He is my brother and I will take care of him.'

'Alright,' said Jacob. 'Take him along and I will pray for God to take care of you all.'

Together the ten brothers set off for Egypt, where everything went much better than they had dared to hope. When they arrived they were taken to the palace of the governor where they saw Simeon. The governor was very friendly indeed. Joseph was extremely happy to see his little brother Benjamin. He was so happy he began to cry and hurried into another room so that the brothers couldn't see his tears. Joseph blew his nose, dried his tears and went back to speak with his brothers.

He invited them to eat at the palace. Benjamin came too and he was given the best food and the largest helping. They also had delicious wine to drink. Joseph drank from a very fine silver cup.

Later, in the middle of the night, when the brothers were sleeping, Joseph had the empty bags filled again, but this time secretly slipped the silver cup into Benjamin's sack. The brothers were unaware of what he had done.

Early next morning they set out for home with food for their families, feeling very pleased with themselves. All had gone well with Benjamin and they had Simeon with them too. They walked fast to get home to Jacob as soon as possible with the good news.

Suddenly they heard shouting behind them! A band of soldiers came running after them. The first soldier shouted, 'Stop! Wait there! Why have you been so dishonest? Why have you stolen the silver cup of the governor?'

The brothers were frightened at first but then they grew angry. They said, 'What do you think we are? Thieves? We haven't stolen anything. Search our bags! You may do what you like with the man who has the governor's silver cup.'

'Alright,' said the soldiers. 'The one who has the cup goes back with us to the governor.'

So the soldiers looked and found the silver cup in Benjamin's sack. 'I didn't steal the cup. I don't know how it got into my bag!', cried Benjamin. No matter how much he protested it did no good. The soldiers grabbed him and took him back with them. The brothers wouldn't leave Benjamin at a time like this so they also went back with the soldiers. When they all stood before the governor he was no longer friendly. He was stern and angry, just as he had been the first time the brothers had come to Egypt.

'Go away,' he said to the brothers. 'Benjamin is the only one who has to stay here.' But the brothers wouldn't go! They loved their youngest brother, and Judah cared for him the most. Judah said, 'Sir, please let Benjamin go home! Our old father will die broken-hearted if something happens to him. Let Benjamin go and punish me. I promised father I would take care of him.'

Then Joseph knew his brothers had changed and he could continue the deception no longer. He sobbed as he told them, 'I am Joseph! I am Joseph!' Then he asked, 'Is my father still alive?'

Never had the brothers been so surprised! Could it be possible this was the same Joseph whom they had teased so much; the one they had sold to the traders? Was Joseph really the stern governor they were facing at this moment? They shook with fear because they were afraid that he would get even with them for the things they had done.

'Don't be afraid,' Joseph told them. 'I am not angry with you anymore. You have done wrong but God has made all things right again, and I have forgiven

you everything. Had I not come to Egypt you wouldn't have had any food for your families.'

He kissed Benjamin and all the others and then he sent them home quickly to Jacob. He also gave them fine presents to take along including a coach for Jacob to ride in. He told them, 'You must come back with my father and live here in Egypt. I will see that you always have enough food to eat.'

Everything had turned out well. No soldiers came after them this time to take them back to the governor and the journey home was a happy one.

Jacob comes to Egypt

Jacob was standing near his tent, his hand shading his eyes as he watched for his sons' return. He was very pleased to see them all, including Benjamin. God had heard his prayer.

'Father, Joseph is still alive!' they called out to him as they came closer. 'He is the governor in Egypt!'

Jacob couldn't believe them and his face became pale with shock. He couldn't believe his dearest son, Joseph, was still alive. Could it be possible that he was now such a great man? But when his sons told him everything and showed him the lovely presents including the beautiful coach Joseph had sent to him, Jacob had to believe them. He laughed and cried at the same time.

'I'll go along,' he cried. 'Oh yes, I'm going back with you to Egypt. My son Joseph is still alive and I will see him before I die.'

Shortly after this they all went together on the long journey to Egypt. The Lord had told him, 'Jacob, you may go in peace. I will take care of you.' Judah went ahead to tell Joseph his father was coming. When Jacob came close to Egypt, Joseph rode out in his own beautiful coach to meet him. As soon as he saw his father, he jumped from the coach, ran, threw his arms around him and kissed him.

'Oh, father! Father!' cried Joseph over and over.

'Joseph, my dear, dear son,' said Jacob.

They both cried for joy.

'Now that I have seen you again,' said Jacob, 'I can die in peace.'

Jacob settled with all his children in the land of Egypt, where Joseph was governor. They moved to a part of the country called Goshen. Joseph had saved them all from death for, had he not been the governor of Egypt, they would surely have died from hunger during the famine. Now they were all in Egypt with him and Joseph took good care of them and they all lived happily together.

M oses

Many years after Jacob and all his sons had died, there lived a father and mother in the land of Goshen. They had three children. The first was a big girl called Miriam. The second was a boy whose name was Aaron; he was about three years old. The third was a baby boy.

The father and mother were very happy with Miriam and Aaron, but they were not at all happy when the new baby came because they knew that they would not be allowed to keep him. A new king was now ruling the land, who knew nothing about Joseph. He didn't know that Joseph had saved the entire country from hunger and death. Jacob, Joseph and all his brothers had died but their children had remained in Goshen. At first they had been a small group, but as time went by more babies were born. The children grew into men and women who also had children, and now they had become a great nation, called the children of Israel, which was another name given to Jacob.

The new king was very afraid of the people of Israel. He thought, 'Those people are growing too strong. Soon they will be stronger than the Egyptians and then they will try to rule us. This must never happen.' This was why all the baby boys who were born to the Israelites were to be drowned. The people must not grow too large or too strong. To keep their numbers down he ordered that all the baby boys were to be thrown into the river Nile.

The father and mother loved their baby too much and couldn't do this dreadful thing. Besides, they knew God wouldn't want them to do it. They hid their new baby in a dark corner of the house so that no-one would find him. They warned Miriam and Aaron, 'You must not tell anyone you have a baby brother! If the king should hear about it he will send soldiers to take our baby away and throw him into the river.' Miriam and Aaron kept the secret.

The baby's father and all the other men in Goshen had to work for the king. Early each morning he had to go to work to make bricks. With the bricks they built walls, houses and palaces. They had to build an entire city. Whoever didn't work hard enough was beaten. The people grumbled about it but it didn't help at all as the king was their master.

Nobody knew there was a baby boy in that little house in Goshen. His mother kept him very safe for three long months. Sometimes the baby would cry long and hard and as he grew stronger, his cry became louder too. His cry could be heard out in the street and it became very hard to hide him. The soldiers of the king walked up and down the streets outside the houses so the parents were afraid that they would hear the baby and take him away.

Then they had an idea. The mother went down to the river where she picked twigs and reeds from along the bank. Then she took them home where she wove them into a basket. She closed the cracks between the reeds with pitch until it looked like a cradle. When it was finished she put the baby inside and took the basket outdoors. Miriam went with her mother to the river where the Egyptians drowned the baby boys. Wading into the water she carefully placed the basket between the reeds at the river's edge, where the water wasn't very deep.

The little basket now looked like a small boat as it floated on the water. In the basket lay the baby, fast asleep. The mother looked up to heaven, and said, 'Dear Lord, you will have to take care of my child, for I cannot do it anymore. If you watch over my baby, I know that he will be safe from harm.'

Then she went home, leaving Miriam hiding in the bushes where she could keep an eye on the basket with her baby brother. It was very warm and still on the water. The sun was shining and the little basket rocked to and fro on the waves but nothing else happened for a long time.

One day when she was down at the river's edge, Miriam heard voices and footsteps. She peeped through the bushes to see who was coming. She saw a beautiful lady strolling along with her maids. It was the princess, the daughter of the king. It was a very warm day and she was looking for a nice place to bathe in the cool water of the river. As she walked along the river bank she saw the basket.

'Oh, look! What is that? Go and fetch it for me,' she ordered. One of her maids went into the water to get the basket and, just as she picked it up, the baby woke and started to cry. When the princess saw the crying baby she felt sorry for it.

'What a dear little baby,' she said. 'It must be a little boy of the people of Israel, but this one won't be drowned. I have found him and he will become my son. I shall call him Moses; a good name for him, because it means "Taken out of the water".'

All this time the baby kept crying because he was hungry and needed his mother's milk. The princess couldn't nurse him, nor could her maids. Just then Miriam came out of the bushes. She had heard everything they had said and asked, 'Shall I get a woman who can nurse the baby?'

'Please do,' said the princess. 'Go quickly.'

Miriam ran fast and called her mother. When they returned, the princess asked, 'Will you nurse this baby?'

'Yes, princess,' said the mother.

'Take him home with you then. Keep him and take good care of him. I will pay you until he is older and can feed himself. Then I must have him back as my son.'

'Very well, princess,' said Moses' mother.

God had heard her prayers and had cared for her baby. Moses would live and she would even receive money to look after him. She no longer had to hide Moses in a dark corner, nor be afraid that the soldiers would come and take him away. Everyone in the family was happy because of what God had done for them.

oses becomes a Prince

Moses stayed with his mother for some time. He played with his brother and sister every day and learned to walk and talk. Moses learned from his mother all about Jacob and Joseph and the children of Israel who lived in Goshen. Then came a very sad day when Moses had to move to the palace to live with the princess, and be brought up as an Egyptian.

Now the princess was his mother and he became a prince. He was given different clothes and lived in an Egyptian palace. But Moses knew that the princess was not his real mother. He remembered that his mother was poor and lived in a little house. He remembered how she had often taken him on her lap and told him wonderful stories about the God of Israel.

Prince Moses grew fast. He became a man and lived in his own palace, with servants, horses and coaches. Whenever he walked in the street, the people bowed very reverently on their knees. 'Look,' they would say, 'the son of the princess!'

Whenever Moses heard them, he would shake his head and think, 'No, I am not the son of the princess! I don't want to be her son. I am the son of a poor woman of the people of Israel!'

'I don't belong here,' he thought. 'I don't belong to the Egyptians, I belong to the people of Israel, for they are the people of God!'

One day Moses went for a walk to the neighbourhood where he was born, to the houses where his people lived. The Egyptians continued to force the

Israelites to make bricks and build houses. Whoever didn't work hard enough was still beaten.

Suddenly he heard a man cry out. He probably hadn't worked hard enough and now he was being whipped by a cruel Egyptian. No matter how loudly the poor man cried and moaned, the Egyptian paid no attention and had no pity on him. Moses was angry with what he saw. Looking around quickly, he saw no one standing close by so he jumped on top of the Egyptian and beat him to death.

Now the Egyptian could never again harm the people of Israel, for he lay dead on the ground. But Moses knew that he had to move the body for no one must know what he had done, especially the king. As fast as he could, Moses dug a hole in the ground, put the man in it and filled it with sand as if nothing had happened.

When he went for a walk the next day he heard shouting. Was someone else being beaten by another Egyptian? But this time it was two men of Israel quarrelling and fighting. He tried to stop the fight but one of the men looked at him rudely and said, 'It is none of your business. You are not our boss.' Then he added, 'Maybe you want to kill me as you killed the Egyptian yesterday.' Moses was shocked when he heard this for he thought that no one had seen him. Perhaps everybody knew about it now, perhaps even the king!

The king had heard about it, and sent soldiers to arrest Moses for murder. So Moses fled away across the desert where he thought no one would find him.He became a wanderer. He had wanted to help the children of Israel but

there seemed to be nothing that he could do now. But God saw it all and he alone could help the people of Israel. Moses had to wait quietly for God's time.

Moses becomes a Shepherd

After wandering in the desert for a long time, Moses finally came to a country with many high mountains, called Midian. One evening he came to a well, a deep hole in the ground with clear water in it. He sat down on the edge of the well to rest and while he was there, seven girls came with a large flock of sheep. They had come to give their sheep water. They lifted the water out of the well with their jugs and poured it into a large stone basin from which the sheep could drink with ease.

Suddenly some men came along with more sheep. They rudely chased the girls away from the water. 'Get out of our way,' they said. 'Our sheep must drink first. You'll have to wait until we're finished.'

The girls were afraid of the men, so they quickly made room for them at the well. But Moses wasn't afraid. When he saw how mean the men were to the girls, he became very angry. Standing in front of the newcomers, he said, 'You men get out of the way fast! These girls were here first and they must give their sheep water first. Don't you dare bother them again!'

Moses called the girls back and helped them with their sheep. Soon the animals were watered and the girls went happily on their way home because they had finished their work so early.

The seven girls were sisters and their father was a priest, an old servant of God. 'My, you're home early tonight,' said the father.

The girls told their father about the man who had helped them at the well.

'And where is the man now?' asked the father.

'Why, he must still be sitting at the well,' answered the girls.

'Shame on you. Hurry and ask this kind man to come and have supper with us tonight.'

So Moses came into the home of the old priest and stayed overnight. Later they asked him to live with them like one of the family. After a while he married one of the seven sisters, whose name was Zipporah.

Moses now had a home and a wife to share his life with. Now he had to earn a living so he helped with the sheep which belonged to the family. Each day he would go into the fields with the sheep to find rich green grass for them. Each evening he would bring them to the well to let them drink. Whenever wild animals came to hurt the sheep, Moses would chase them away.

How Moses had changed! Once he had been a wealthy prince but now he was a poor shepherd. Once his life had been easy but now he had to work hard each day, looking after sheep. He used to be quick-tempered and hot-headed, because he had wanted to help his people, but now he was learning to be patient.

Moses waited a long time for God to help the people of Israel. For forty years he worked as a shepherd, tending the family sheep and nothing happened. He hardly thought about

his people any more. In fact, he had almost forgotten them as he grew older. But God hadn't forgotten the people of Israel.

One day as Moses walked in the field with the sheep he saw a very strange thing happening. A large bush was burning. This wasn't a very unusual thing in the desert, as there were fires from time to time, but this particular bush didn't seem to be burning up. Although there were flames, the leaves and branches on the bush remained as green as ever.

'I must take a closer look,' thought Moses, 'for this is a miracle!' As he walked closer, he heard a voice come out of the flames.

'Moses, Moses!' called the voice.

Moses was both surprised and frightened. He answered, 'Here I am...!'

And the voice said, 'You may not come any closer, Moses, for I am here. I am the God of Abraham, Isaac, and Jacob.'

Hearing this, Moses fell on his knees and listened to what the Lord had to tell him. He didn't dare look up while God told him he now wanted to help the people of Israel. The Lord wanted to bring them to the Promised

Land. Moses was to go to the king of Egypt and tell him he must let the Israelites go.

Moses had changed a lot in the forty years he had tended sheep. Once Moses had dared to do all kinds of things but now he didn't care to go to the king at all! Moses would much prefer God to send another man to Egypt and leave him alone to remain a shepherd. But the Lord told Moses he had to go, and he didn't dare say, 'No' to God.

The Lord told Moses he would help and protect him and told him to take his brother Aaron along with him. Suddenly everything grew quiet again. The voice no longer spoke and the bush didn't burn any more. It was as though nothing had happened!

Moses brought his sheep to their fold and went home. Someone else would have to care for them now because he could no longer do it himself. The Lord had given him other work to do. He would be allowed to help bring his people to the Promised Land. Moses then started on the long trip back to Egypt. Now he was no longer afraid for he knew God would watch over him.

M oses returns to Egypt

Moses' return to Egypt was a long tiring journey. On the way, a man as old as Moses came out to meet him. It was his brother, Aaron. Moses was so happy to see his brother again after all these years that he threw his arms round him and kissed him. Then he told him all that the Lord had said from the burning bush as they made their way towards Egypt.

First they went to the people of Israel and told them the Lord was going to set them free to live in a land he had promised to them. The heavy work and all the cruel punishment would soon be over. They were very happy and thanked God.

Moses and Aaron then went to the king who lived in a beautiful palace. He sat on a golden chair in a magnificent room looking very proud, and around him were many servants. Moses and Aaron were not afraid. They knew the Lord was watching over them as they stood before the king. They said, 'The Lord, the God of Israel says: "Let my people go out of Egypt".'

The king was angry and said, 'No, the people of Israel must stay here, to work for me.'

'But the Lord himself has said it,' replied Moses and Aaron. 'Surely you have to obey God.'

The king became furious and shouted, 'I don't know the Lord, and I don't want to obey him, either! I'll have nothing to do with your God. I'm the ruler over these people and will continue to be so. From now on I'll make them work harder than ever before, and if they don't finish their work, I'll have them beaten twice as hard as before. Go away and get on with your own work.'

So they left, but they were very sad, for everything was now even worse than before. Surely, if the Lord were not with Moses and Aaron, the people would never be able to leave Egypt! But Moses and Aaron were not alone, for God was with them. He would see to it that the king would obey his orders. The Lord would punish him for his disobedience by sending ten terrible plagues to the king and the Egyptian people.

First of all the water in Egypt changed to blood so that the people had nothing to drink. After that a great many frogs were everywhere, skipping and hopping all around. They were in all the rooms of the Egyptians' houses and even jumped into the food and onto the people's beds.

The king became frightened so he called Moses and Aaron and said, 'I will let the people go, but first you must take these awful frogs away.'

Moses was glad, and he prayed to the Lord. All the frogs died and the plague was over, but as soon as the king saw this, he was no longer afraid. He said, 'Yes, I promised I would let the people go, but I have changed my mind. All the people must remain here.'

Then another punishment came. The dust on the earth changed to lice which bit the Egyptians. In addition to the lice, swarms of flies came to bother the people. There was no place to hide from the pests. Again the king promised to let the people of Israel go but, as soon as the plague was gone, he went back on his word.

The plagues became worse. All the animals in Egypt grew sick. The cows and the sheep died, but the animals of the Israelites remained healthy. The people of Egypt them-selves grew ill with big painful boils all over their bodies.

Then there was a big hailstorm.

The wheat was beaten to the ground, leaves were torn from the trees and the people caught in the hailstorm were killed. Yet the king still wouldn't obey.

Grasshoppers came! They were only small insects but they came in swarms like huge clouds. There were so many grasshoppers in the air it grew dark in the middle of the day. Everywhere the grasshoppers landed they would eat all the grass and leaves. They ate and ate until all the crops in the fields disappeared. Still the king wouldn't obey!

Then it grew so dark one couldn't see a thing. Even though it was the middle of the day, the sun didn't shine. It was just like night and it lasted three days. The people sat huddled close together in their houses, very afraid. Even the king in his palace was afraid but still he wouldn't obey God!

Then came the last plague, which was to be the most terrible of all. It was evening and the people of Egypt were going to bed. They had no idea of what was about to happen. That particular evening, however, the people of Israel were not getting ready for bed. They were all dressed and ready to leave, with all the things they wanted to take with them packed in preparation. The Lord had told Moses that the people would start their long journey to Canaan that very night.

First the Israelites must eat their last meal in Egypt. Each family baked bread and prepared a fresh lamb. The bread and the lambs were placed on the tables. It was to be a great feast for Israel, for that night they were to become free people. Each father took the lamb's blood outside, and with brushes made from leaves, they painted the blood on the door posts. They put the blood on the left and on the right side and also above the door. In each home of the Israelites they did the same thing until every door became red with blood. Then night fell.

During this last night came the final terrible punishment. An angel came down from heaven and went through the streets into every Egyptian home and wherever he went, the oldest son died in his sleep. Even the king's house was not passed by.

But when the angel came to the houses of the people of Israel he didn't go in. Whenever he came to a door marked with the blood of a lamb he passed by the house. The Lord had told the angel that when he saw blood on the door, he must not go in. The sign of the blood saved the people of Israel. That night the people of Israel celebrated.

The Egyptians, however, were not celebrating, for they were terribly sad because a son had died in every home. Everyone was afraid and the king had no choice but to let the people of Israel go. 'Let those people go!' he shouted.

The Egyptians went to the people of Israel and gave them all kinds of beautiful things made of gold and silver. 'Here,' they said. 'You may have all these things but you must go away quickly!'

When morning came, the people of Israel started their long journey with their children, their animals and all the gifts from the frightened Egyptians. At last they were on their way to the promised land of Canaan.

M oses leads his people through the sea

The journey to Canaan was a long one, and the people of Israel would have to walk all the way. There were many children and animals so they had to travel very slowly. Never before had the people of Israel been so far away from Egypt. They hadn't any idea where they were going. They knew of course, that they were on their way to the Promised Land, but they didn't know how to get there. So they followed Moses as he led the way with God's help.

In the blue sky a white cloud floated ahead of the Israelites. This was the cloud of the Lord and it showed them the way. God himself was travelling with them into this strange land. The Lord took good care of his people. When the sun became so hot that it burned the skin of the people, the Lord would cover it with his cloud and the air grew cool again. Whenever the children grew too tired the cloud stopped and allowed them to rest.

In the evenings, when the sun set, it did not grow dark, for there was a flame in the cloud, which gave some light. God promised to lead and protect them.

After three days of travelling, the people of Israel came to the sea. As they neared the shore they heard a great noise behind them , and when they turned they saw clouds of dust as horses and chariots thundered towards them. The Egyptians were coming after them; the king had changed his mind again. The king was sorry he had allowed the Israelites to leave his country and he was coming with his soldiers to force them back to Egypt. The people were terrified for they could go no further. In front of them was the sea and behind them were well-armed soldiers. They cried and wailed in fear.

Moses shouted, 'Don't be afraid! The Lord is with us. Come along and follow me. You won't have to fight the soldiers because the Lord will fight for you. Just be quiet and come along.'

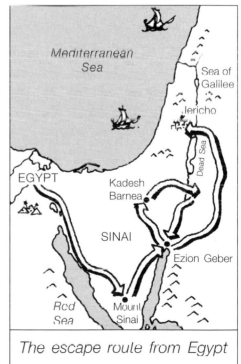

When the people heard this, they did as they were told and followed Moses towards the sea. The water was very deep and the waves roared against the shore but Moses lifted his staff high above the water. A wind came and blew the water aside.

Soon a path was formed right through the sea, with the water on either side like a great wall. Moses walked straight on between the walls of water where there was dry land. Behind him marched all the people of Israel.

The escape route from Egypt

The cloud followed behind the people, between them and the soldiers. It meant, 'Don't be afraid, I am watching over you.' On the side of the people of Israel, the cloud gave light, but on the side facing the Egyptian soldiers, it was dark.

Soon the king and his soldiers reached the sea. They looked around wondering where the Israelites had gone. Then they saw them in the middle of the sea between the walls of water.

The king and his soldiers were so angry they didn't stop to think what a great miracle it was. 'Forward!' shouted the king. 'We'll get them yet! We'll show them!'

The king rode into the sea on his chariot followed by his soldiers. They rode as fast as they could trying to catch up with the Israelites, but they couldn't see in the darkness of the cloud that passed in front of them.

When morning came the people of Israel had reached the other side of the sea, but the Egyptians were still in the middle. The Lord said to Moses, 'Now stretch out your hand over the water.'

Moses stretched out his hand and the water flowed back over the path of the Egyptians, covering the horses and chariots of the king and his soldiers until they all drowned.

The king and his soldiers had done terrible things to the people of Israel but they would never harm them again.

At last the people of Israel were free. They celebrated by the side of the sea and sang to thank the Lord:

> *'Sing to the Lord, for he is highly exalted.*
> *The horse and the rider he has thrown into the sea.'*

M oses leads his people through the desert

The people of Israel had walked safely through the middle of the Red Sea, but the king and all his soldiers died when the waters closed over them. Now the people were free and they could travel on in peace to the Promised Land. The people would not lose their way through the strange countryside because the Lord would show them where to go.

Sometimes the Israelites forgot God's promise. After a short while they began to grumble when everything didn't run as smoothly as they thought it should. When things didn't go well they became afraid and forgot that the Lord was with them.

The Israelites came to a desert which they had to cross. There was nothing but sand and stones and it was very hot. The older people and the children grew thirsty from walking through the hot sand, but there were no wells or streams from which to get water.

One day they came across a pool of water and they ran over to drink, but it had a terrible taste! It was so bitter they couldn't drink it. The Israelites began to grumble and complain to Moses. 'What are we going to drink now?'

Moses quietly took a piece of wood and threw it into the water, as the Lord had told him to do. 'Now drink!' he said. 'The water is alright now.' Sure enough, the bitter water had suddenly become fresh and sweet. Of course the wood alone hadn't done this, nor had Moses. Only the Lord has the power to do such a thing. Surely the Israelites would now believe God's promise to look after them.

A few days later all the bread and meat they had taken out of Egypt was finished. When they had nothing left to eat they began to grumble again.

'In Egypt we had enough food to eat so why didn't you leave us there? Why did you take us away to let us die of hunger here in the desert?'

Moses told them not to grumble. 'The Lord will take care of you. Tonight he is going to give you meat and tomorrow he will send bread from heaven. Then will you believe that he cares for you?'

That evening a huge flock of birds came flying towards them. They were big fat birds called quail. They were so tired of flying that they fell to the ground between the tents where the Israelites were camping. They picked up the birds and cooked them over their fires. They had as much meat as they wanted to eat.

The next morning when the people went outside the ground was white, as if it had snowed overnight. There were countless tiny round white flakes.

'What is it?' asked the people.

'It is manna,' Moses explained. 'Bread which the Lord has given us to eat.'

The people gathered it as fast as they could, scooping up handfuls and jugfuls - as much as they could eat. They were able to eat it raw, bake it into cakes or cook it as a sort of porridge. It tasted good and each morning there was plenty for the people to gather.

Now they knew that they would never again have to suffer hunger, and were sure the Lord would take care of all their needs. Surely they would now learn to trust in God. Sadly however, their faith was very weak. Once again, when they ran out of water they were very angry with Moses and blamed him for it.

'Lord, what shall I do?' he prayed.

The Lord told Moses to go to a large rock which was enclosed by the camp and strike it with his staff. With all the people following him, shouting and

complaining, Moses did as the Lord had said and the stone split open. A stream of cold water flowed out and the people were quiet as they rushed over to quench their thirst.

Later another wonderful thing happened. The Israelites could surely tell that God was watching over his people. A big band of thieves who lived in the desert came to steal and rob from them. Moses realised that he would have to do something about it. He called on Joshua, a young man who was a good fighter but who, more importantly, loved the Lord.

'This can't go on any longer. Pick out the strongest of our men to fight the robbers and give them such a beating that they'll never dare to come back again.'

When Joshua and his men went out to fight the thieves, Moses climbed a nearby hill to watch the battle and to pray to the Lord to help them. Stretching out his hands towards heaven, he called, 'Lord, please help us!'

As he continued to pray, keeping his hands held up high, the Lord heard him and the Israelites defeated the enemy. Once again, God had blessed them and had answered their prayers.

The Golden Calf

The people of Israel travelled on, with the white cloud still ahead of them to show the way. They reached the country where Moses had lived for a long time as a shepherd and the cloud stopped over the top of a high mountain called Sinai. When they came to the foot of the mountain the Israelites decided to stay there for a while. The Lord had told them that he was going to meet them there and that something special would happen.

Everyone put on their best clothes and early in the morning of that special day, they stood waiting close to the mountain. As the cloud hung over the summit they heard the sound of thunder and the whole mountain began to shake and tremble. Then it became very quiet and all the people heard the voice of God speaking to them. He told them that they must always obey him, love him above all others, and love one another also. God gave them ten commandments, rules by which they should lead their lives. Provided they obeyed the Lord they would be blessed, and would be the happiest people in the world.

Later, the thunder started again and everyone ran back to their tents, for they were afraid to stay too close to the mountain. This time Moses climbed to the top of Sinai to write down everything the Lord had said, so that the Israelites would never forget his words. The people looked out of their tents and watched him go higher and higher until finally he disappeared into the cloud on the summit.

That evening they watched and waited for Moses to return, but darkness fell and there was no sign of him. Neither did he appear the following day. When he had not come back after a further two days on the mountain the people began to worry and said, 'Perhaps Moses will never return! Maybe he has had an accident up there and he is dead. Who will take us to Canaan if we have no one to lead us?'

Then some of them began to say, 'We cannot see God anyway, so perhaps he has left us too. Other nations have an image of their god, in front of which they can kneel and pray, so why can't we have one to worship? Let us make a golden image which we can carry with us to Canaan.'

So they went to Aaron, who was left in charge while Moses was away. 'Make us an image, a god we can see and carry with us to the Promised Land.'

IDOLATRY

is worshipping a false god, loving something more than God himself.

In Bible times people often made idols to different gods, hoping to please them.

God hates idolatry

One of his commandments is:
You shall have no other gods before me.
You shall not make yourself an idol.

The commandments are found in Exodus, chapter 20.

Aaron was taken aback at their suggestion, but the crowd seemed angry and he was afraid of what they would do if he refused. So he told them to bring all the gold they had in rings and other jewellery so that he could melt it down and mould it into an idol. To his surprise the people were willing to hand their gold over to him, and he did what they had asked, making a large golden calf similar to what they had seen in Egypt. Then the Israelites could kneel before it to pray.

The people were delighted and began to shout and dance for joy around the golden calf. The noise was so great that it could be heard on the top of Mount Sinai. As they were shouting and dancing, suddenly a man stepped into the centre of the crowd. It was Moses, back from the top of the mountain! He wasn't afraid of the people as Aaron had been and he was very angry with them. As the crowd watched, Moses took the golden calf, turned it upside down and then burned it on a blazing fire until there was nothing left of the idol. Then the people were worried when they realised how they had sinned against God. They began to wonder whether God would ever forgive them.

The next day Moses climbed the mountain again, but he was sad and afraid this time when he knelt before the Lord: 'Oh Lord, these people have done a great sin and deserve a terrible punishment, but please remain their friend. Let me take the punishment in their place.'

Despite what they had done, and although they had disobeyed the Lord, he still loved the children of Israel and wanted them to be his people. God loved them much more than Moses ever possibly could.

T he Israelites doubt God again

The Israelites lived near the slopes of Mount Sinai for nearly a year before the time came for them to continue on their way to Canaan. Each day they came a little closer to the Promised Land, until one day they were able to catch sight of the mountains of Canaan in the distance. Then the cloud stopped and they set up camp to rest for a few days before continuing into the new land.

Now at that time, other people were living in Canaan who did not worship the God of Israel. Before Moses could lead his people into the Promised Land there

were many things he had to find out. He wanted to know how many people lived there and how strong their armies were. Then he had to learn if there was good grazing for the cattle, and plenty of food for the people to eat. In fact, he had to find out whether the land was indeed as wonderful as everyone hoped it would be.

Moses chose twelve brave and strong men to go into Canaan as spies. One of them was Joshua, whose army fought and defeated the robbers who attacked the Israelites. Moses told them, 'You must climb those mountains and go into the land of Canaan. There you must have a good look at everything before coming back to tell us what you saw. Be careful that the Canaanites don't catch you!'

The next day the twelve men set out for the Promised Land. The Israelites waited impatiently for their return as they were eager to hear all about Canaan.

After what seemed a long time, the twelve men came back to the camp, bringing with them many things to show the people. They carried all kinds of delicious fruit: apples, juicy figs and large clusters of grapes which were so heavy two men had to carry them between them, tied to a stick over their shoulders.

'If Canaan has beautiful fruit like this,' said the Israelites, 'it must be a wonderful country!'

Joshua and Caleb, two of the twelve men who really loved the Lord, reported that it was a wonderful country and that they believed that God would lead them safely there. But the other ten didn't have faith in God. They said, 'There are flowers and fruit everywhere and plenty of grass for our cattle, but we cannot go into Canaan. The people who live there are far too strong for us. We even saw giants, so tall that we felt like puppets next to them. We will never be able to defeat them.'

The Israelites grew afraid when they heard the news. Once again they had forgotten the Lord who watched over them and the thought of the giants scared them even more. But Joshua and Caleb trusted the Lord and told the people, 'Don't be afraid! The Lord will help us for he has promised to give us that country and we believe he will. You must believe it too.'

But they didn't believe that God would lead them into Canaan. Instead they began to moan and complain, grumbling against God and Moses. 'If only we had stayed in Egypt. Why did God bring us here to let us be killed by giants? There is no way we will go into the land of Canaan. Let's go back to Egypt.'

Joshua and Caleb tried to reason with them but the people didn't pay any attention. They became so angry with Joshua and Caleb that they tried to kill them. They were on the point of stoning them to death when God stepped in to save them. A glaring white light came from the cloud like a bolt of lightning from heaven. The crowd screamed in terror, covering their faces from the dazzling light and fell back shaking with fear.

'As a punishment for failing to trust

the Lord,' Moses told them, 'He has said that you shall not enter into Canaan but shall wander in the desert until your children have grown up. Then they will enter the land of Canaan instead of you. All except Joshua and Caleb, who believed in the Lord, will die in the desert.'

Despite this warning some of them wanted to enter the Promised Land. The next morning they came to Moses and said, 'Yesterday we were disobedient and afraid but now we want to go into Canaan and will fight bravely against the people who live there.'

Moses shook his head sadly and told them, 'Don't go. God will not allow you to enter Canaan.'

The men decided to go anyway. Though they fought bravely the Lord didn't help them and they were all killed by the Canaanites. The others turned back and the cloud led the way again. But as they journeyed into the desert, further away from the Promised Land, their heads were bent down and their hearts were full of sadness.

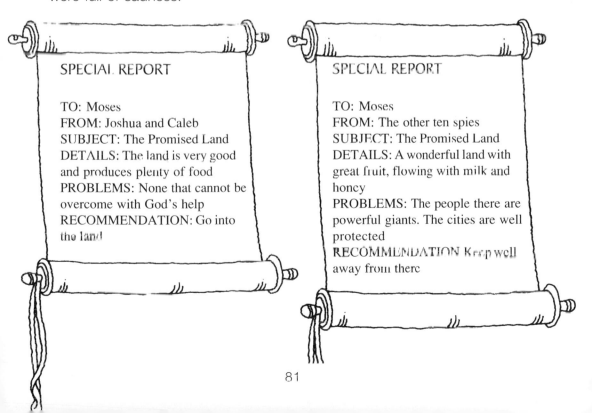

SPECIAL REPORT

TO: Moses
FROM: Joshua and Caleb
SUBJECT: The Promised Land
DETAILS: The land is very good and produces plenty of food
PROBLEMS: None that cannot be overcome with God's help
RECOMMENDATION: Go into the land

SPECIAL REPORT

TO: Moses
FROM: The other ten spies
SUBJECT: The Promised Land
DETAILS: A wonderful land with great fruit, flowing with milk and honey
PROBLEMS: The people there are powerful giants. The cities are well protected
RECOMMENDATION: Keep well away from there

ravelling through the desert

The Israelites continued deeper into the desert until they had left the land of Canaan far behind them. It was a sad journey and all the more so because they continued to grumble and complain. When they had difficulty finding water they put the blame on Moses and Aaron: 'Why did you bring us here? It's your fault we're so thirsty!'

As he had done once before, Moses went over to a rock which God had shown him would provide them with water. Shouting and grumbling, the people followed Moses and Aaron to the rock. Moses lost his temper: 'Listen, you disobedient people! Shall we let water gush out of this rock for you?' And he struck the rock hard twice in a fit of anger! Water gushed out and everyone rushed forward to drink.

Everyone was happy for a short time but Moses and Aaron regretted their quick temper for it was as if they had not believed that God would look after them. So God told Moses and Aaron, 'Because you have forgotten me, you may not enter the land of Canaan either.'

The manna which the Lord provided for them appeared every morning as before, but after a while the people began to complain about it: 'Manna, every day the same!' as they kicked it into the sand when they found it.

God was not pleased with their attitude and things got worse for them. One day poisonous snakes came crawling into the tents and bit the people. Many died, and when there was nothing that anyone could do about it everyone became afraid. They went to Moses and pleaded, 'Please help us. Please pray to God for his forgiveness and please ask him to take away the horrible snakes.'

So Moses prayed and the Lord heard him. But instead of taking the snakes away, God worked a miracle. Moses gathered the people together. Holding a long stick on top of which was a snake made of copper, he told them that if they were bitten, they were to look up at it and they wouldn't die. In this way God wanted to teach the people that they must always trust him and look to him for help. If they did so they would have nothing to fear.

M oses goes to be with God

After many years of wandering through the desert their long journey was almost over and the people of Israel came close to the land of Canaan. Many of the older people had died and their children had grown up, but after all this time they wondered how they would actually get into the Promised Land. Would the Lord help them to defeat the people who were there?

The Promised Land lay ahead of the Israelites. In the distance they could see the mountains and it wouldn't be long before they could enter. But Moses couldn't go any further with them as God had told him that he would not go into Canaan because of his disobedience. His brother Aaron had already died.

Moses prayed once more to the Lord, hoping he might be allowed to go into Canaan with the people of Israel: 'Oh Lord, I don't deserve it but I want so much to go into the land you promised us. I would be so happy if I could see the land where our people will live.'

But it was not to be. Moses still loved the Lord for he remembered all the wonderful ways in which God had protected him from danger: from his birth in Egypt to that moment when he had finally shown the people the way to the land of Canaan. When Moses thought about all that the Lord had done for him he was happy again.

Moses wanted to talk to the people once more so he called them all together. He wanted them to remember that they must always be obedient to the Lord and remain close to him, for only then would they be happy in the new land.

PERSONAL PROFILE

NAME: *Moses*

FAMILY: *From the tribe of Levi. Had one sister called Miriam and a brother called Aaron. His wife's name was Zipporah.*

BACKGROUND: *His early years were spent with his parents. He was later taken to live at the royal palace. After committing murder he ran away from Egypt and lived as a shepherd in Midian, until God called him to rescue the Israelites from slavery in Egypt.*

POINTS OF INTEREST: *'Moses' is an Egyptian name which means 'drawn out of water'.*

Moses told them what would happen if they forgot the Lord. They would be unhappy and wouldn't be allowed to remain in Canaan.

Then Moses said goodbye to the Israelites and walked away alone towards a nearby mountain. As the people watched, he climbed higher and higher until he disappeared out of sight.

When Moses reached the top of the mountain the Lord came to join him. Moses could see a great distance from the mountain top. He could see the fertile land where his people were soon to live, and God showed him the green pastures and the rivers which ran through them. He showed him the mountains, the trees and the sea beyond. Moses saw the whole country and knew that the people of Israel were going to be very happy there.

Then the Lord took him to be with himself in heaven, to a land far more beautiful than Canaan.

As both Aaron and Moses were no longer with the Israelites to lead them into the Promised Land, Joshua, the brave soldier, took charge. It was not to be an easy task for Joshua. He knew he would have to be very careful, for there were still many wicked people to be defeated in the land of Canaan before they could enter.

R ahab

The first place they had to conquer was Jericho, a city with a strong wall around it. Before Joshua could lead the people any further he had to find out more about Jericho. How thick and strong were the walls and how many soldiers were in the city? So he called two men and told them, 'I want you to go into the land of Canaan. Go very quietly and enter the city of Jericho. You must see everything you can and then come back to tell me all about it. The Lord will watch over you.'

Bravely they set out and soon reached Jericho. The wall was too high for them to climb over. Set in the wall was a large gate and people were going in and out. The two men mingled with the crowd and walked through the gate without anybody noticing them. Once inside the city they walked through the streets, looking at everything very carefully.

When evening came and it grew dark the two men had to find somewhere to sleep. They walked round the city along the top of the wall and came to a house built into it. When the men knocked at the door they met a woman called Rahab who was willing to give them a bed for the night.

Some of the men in the city had seen the two strangers go into Rahab's house and quickly ran to tell the king, who sent soldiers to arrest the spies. The soldiers banged on the door: 'Rahab, open the door! Where are the strangers? They are enemies, who have come to spy on our land and we have come to take them.'

FLAX

A plant which is used to make linen.

Flax stalks have to be pulled and then dried.

The drying often takes place on the roof tops of houses.

Like the red blood painted on the doorposts at the Passover, the red cord used to identify Rahab's house would keep the people within safe.

What would Rahab do now? Should she let the soldiers in and hand the spies over to them? But Rahab had already hidden the men on top of the flat roof under some flax stalks. 'If you run fast,' she told the soldiers, 'you'll be able to catch up with them for they were here just a short while ago.'

The soldiers ran off to track down the Israelites. Then Rahab went to the roof and called to the two men. She knew very well who they were because she had heard of the people of Israel before. She also knew that God was with them and this was why she had offered to help them.

'The Lord will surely give you the city and all this country,' she said. 'Your God can do all things. We have heard how he brought your people through the middle of the sea and did many other great things. This is why the people here are so afraid of you and why I have been kind to you. Now I want you to promise me that you will be kind to me. In a little while you will come and take this city away from us. Will you remember me then and ensure no harm comes to me? Will you also remember my father and mother, my brothers and sisters?'

The men promised to protect them and told her to put a red cord outside her window so that the soldiers of Israel would know where she and her family lived. Then they hurried to get away in case the king's soldiers returned to find them in Rahab's house.

Rahab took them into the living room and opened the window. Taking a strong red rope she let one end out over the wall and tied the other end to the window. The two men climbed down the rope and disappeared into the night.

They hid in the mountains for a few days before returning safely back to Joshua.

God had looked after them and made sure Rahab would shelter them, even though she did not know them.

Jericho

A few days later the people of Israel marched towards the walls of the city of Jericho. The inhabitants saw them coming and quickly locked the gates. Then they went to the top of the wall and prepared to defend themselves.

The wall was too thick and strong to be demolished and the gates could not be easily broken down. But the Israelites didn't even try to attack the city. Much to the surprise of the soldiers on top of the wall, the people of Israel just walked around the city in a long parade. They walked around the city only once, then they left.

The next day they came again and walked once more around the city. For five days they did the same, walking once round the walls before going back to their camp. When the Israelites walked around the city on the sixth day the people of Jericho were very puzzled. They laughed about it and said, 'What do they think they are doing? Do they think they can take our city just by walking around it?'

But the Israelites were doing this because God had told Joshua to do it. When the seventh day came the people of Israel came out once again, but this time they kept on marching until they had gone round Jericho seven times. Then they stood still. Suddenly they started to shout and cheer, as if they had already defeated their enemy.

As they cheered, the wall began to crack and crumble until, with a huge crash, all the stones come tumbling down! With no wall to block their way, the people of Israel were able to walk straight into the city and capture it. No one in Jericho was left alive except for Rahab's family whom God had promised to protect.

One part of the wall was left standing: a house with a length of red rope hanging from a window. It was the house of Rahab who had helped the two spies. She was saved with her family and they joined the people of Israel.

The Israelites went much further into Canaan and drove the people out of the land.

After all the cities had been taken they set up home in the Promised Land. They built houses for them- selves, sowed grain on their farms and put cattle and sheep out to graze in the fresh green pastures of Canaan.

WALLS

In Bible times cities had strong, thick walls built around them. They gave protection to the people inside. If enemies were seen coming, the people would close the gates to the city and no one could get in.

The walls were so broad that people could easily walk around on top of them. The bricks were often made from reeds and clay mixed together and left to harden in the sun.

Now they had everything they could possibly want. No longer did they have to suffer thirst, for there was plenty of fresh water and good milk. No longer did they need manna for now they could make their own bread from wheat which they grew; and there was lots of delicious fruit and honey.

Joshua told the Israelites, 'You must always remember that it was the Lord who gave you this land. The people who lived here before used to pray to idols and you must never do this. You must pray to God and love him always. You must obey him and do all that he asks.'

'Yes, we will always do this! The Lord is our God!' they replied.

 ideon

It was summer and the grain had ripened on the farms. Everywhere people were busy harvesting their crops. They would thresh it and grind it into flour from which they would make bread. However, there was some concern because, for a few years, when the wheat was ripe, robbers came to steal it and many people were left without bread. When the farmers were gathering in their crops they were afraid, always having to watch to see if anyone was coming to rob them.

A young man called Gideon was gathering in his crop one day. When he had finished he put some grain into a large trough and began to pound it with a stick to make flour. Then he would quickly put it into sacks. In this way Gideon was able to keep his harvest in a safe place somewhere in the mountains. The robbers wouldn't find it there and Gideon would have grain to make bread.

Gideon loved the Lord and he was pleased that he had been able to look after his grain. But he knew how difficult it must be for the people of Israel.

The problem was that the Israelites had once more forgotten about God and Gideon was sad: 'It's their own fault, for they haven't loved the Lord and obeyed his wishes. They have prayed to an idol, just like the people who lived here before - now thieves come to bother us every year. Perhaps God has sent them to punish us!'

Gideon prayed for God's help: 'Please Lord, chase the thieves away! People are asking but you do not hear us.'

As Gideon prayed he suddenly realised that he was no longer alone. When he looked round he saw a man sitting on a rock under a tree. The man turned and spoke to Gideon. It was an angel who had come to give Gideon a message. The Lord had indeed heard the people crying for help and the angel now told Gideon, 'When the robbers come again you must chase them away!'

Gideon couldn't believe what he had heard. 'But how can I do this? I am so young and the robbers are so strong!' But the angel answered, 'You can do it, Gideon! The Lord is going to help you.' When Gideon heard this, he felt better. He knew that if the Lord would help him he could do what was asked of him.

A short time later the robbers came riding into the country on camels. In their hands they carried long spears to attack the Israelites. The people were very afraid and ran to hide in the mountains. But Gideon stayed behind and blew on his trumpet. This was the signal for all the brave men in Israel to gather together to form a large army to defeat the enemy. But Gideon knew that it was not the strength of the army that would chase the robbers away but God, who had promised to help them.

Nevertheless, Gideon wanted to make sure before he attacked the robbers. He wanted God to give him a sign. He took a sheepskin, which was just like a thick blanket, and put it on the grass. Then he prayed, 'Dear Lord, every morning the grass is wet with drops of dew. Tomorrow morning, however, allow the grass to be dry and the blanket wet. Then I shall know you will help me.'

When he woke the next morning he rushed outside to see what had happened It was exactly as he had asked. The grass was dry and the blanket was soaking wet. Gideon could wring out a whole bowlful of water.

Although Gideon believed the Lord would help him he wanted one more sign. Again he placed the sheepskin on the grass and prayed, 'This time, Lord, let the grass be wet and the blanket dry.'

He went to sleep and when he woke, he found the blanket was dry and the grass wet with dew. Now Gideon knew that there was no doubt that the Lord would help him to defeat the thieves.

Calling his army together he led them straight toward the robbers' camp, but God told them that his army was too big! So Gideon sent most of his men home, just as God had told him. Now there was only a small company left. But Gideon wasn't afraid, for the Lord had told him he would help.

To Gideon's surprise God said, 'You still have too many men with you. Send more of them away.'

Gideon did as he was told and sent more of his men home. Now there was only a very small group of men with him. Could this little band fight against such a large number of the enemy?

Night fell. It was dark and quiet and the thieves were fast asleep in their tents. Gideon and his men crept into the camp and stood in a circle around the tents. Suddenly they began to blow loudly on their trumpets, shattering the quiet of the night! Gideon's men had also brought along bottles which they smashed on the ground making an even greater noise.

Each man carried a piece of burning wood as a torch, which they swung round and round until they burned brightly. It was a strange sight, to see bright lights in the middle of the night on top of the noise of trumpets and breaking bottles. Then Gideon and his men started shouting, 'The sword of the Lord and of Gideon!' as they ran down towards the robbers' tents as fast as they could.

The thieves were frightened. All they could see was that they were surrounded by a circle of advancing light which they believed was an army much stronger than they were. Back and forth they ran, bumping into each other in fright, terrified of the Israelites and of each other. They fought with one another, believing they were fighting a huge army. Not daring to remain in their camp for another minute, they ran for their lives, with Gideon's men chasing after them until they left the country altogether. The robbers did not return.

The Israelites were overjoyed and they all came to thank Gideon. But Gideon told them, 'You mustn't thank me, you must thank the Lord! He answered our prayers and set us free.'

R uth

In the town of Bethlehem, in the land of Canaan, there was a woman called Naomi who lived with her husband and two sons. Naomi's husband worked on his farm, where he sowed wheat in the spring and cut it down as soon as it was ripe. He would then thresh the harvest and bring the wheat kernels home to Naomi to grind into flour.

One year there was no wheat at all. Although Naomi's husband had planted the seeds in the spring there was a drought and the plants had dried up and died, leaving them with no grain to grind. Naomi had no flour to bake bread and the family had nothing to eat. Their neighbours were unable to help as they had no grain either. It was the same all over the country.

So Naomi, her husband and two sons decided to move to another country called Moab, where there was plenty of wheat and nobody was hungry. For many years Naomi lived in Moab but a great deal of sadness came into her life. First her husband died. Her two sons married girls from Moab, one was called Ruth and the other Orpah. Sadly, some time later, her two sons became ill and died. She became a sad, lonely woman. Her grief aged her and her hair turned grey.

'I don't want to stay here any longer,' she said. 'It is better for me to return to my own country, where there is surely enough bread for me to eat by now.'

So Naomi set out to return to Bethlehem in Canaan. The two girls, Ruth and Orpah, kept her company part of the way, because they loved Naomi very dearly and were sorry that she was leaving Moab. She had been a kind and loving mother-in-law to them and she had told them about the God of Israel. When they had travelled some distance, Naomi said to them, 'This is far enough. You had better turn back now. You have both been very kind to me and I hope the Lord will bless you and make you happy.'

First Orpah kissed Naomi and, as she bade farewell, there were tears running down her cheeks. She was sorry to leave Naomi, but she wanted to return to be with her own people in Moab.

Ruth also wept but she didn't want to go back. She loved Naomi too much and decided to stay with her, live in Bethlehem and worship the God of Israel. With the Israelites, Ruth felt she could serve the Lord.

'No, I can never leave you! Your people are my people, your God is my God. I want to remain with you always.'

Naomi was very pleased to have Ruth with her and so they travelled on to Bethlehem together. When they reached Canaan the people saw a great change in Naomi. She had left as a young woman and had returned old and grey. They spoke about the sad old woman who had come back from Moab after so many years, and talked about Ruth who didn't want to leave Naomi to live on her own.

The house in which Naomi had lived so many years before was still there, so they moved back in and made it their home. As it was summer, there was plenty of wheat and everyone was busily harvesting the crops. But poor Naomi hadn't any wheat as nothing had been planted on her land. Without wheat there would be no flour, and without flour there could be no bread. Ruth offered to look for some leftover wheat on the farms where the men were harvesting.

Ruth went to the men working in the field: 'May I pick up the ears of grain which you drop along the way?'

It was common practice for the men to allow the poor to follow behind

and pick up any grain which had dropped, so they told Ruth it was alright. She looked carefully all morning and by lunch time she had gathered quite a lot. The men to whom Ruth had spoken were the servants of a wealthy gentleman called Boaz. On that day he came to see how the work was coming along on his farm. When he saw the young girl looking for grain, he asked, 'Who is that girl?'

'That is Ruth,' his servants told him, 'who came from the land of Moab with old Naomi.'

Boaz had heard many kind things about Ruth and he was glad she had come to his farm. Walking over to her, he said, 'You may come here for wheat every day. I will ask my servants to be kind to you and when you are thirsty they will give you a drink. You don't have to go to any other farms.'

Ruth was very happy indeed. Bowing low before the kind gentleman, she asked, 'Why are you taking such good care of me?'

'Because you have been kind to Naomi,' answered Boaz.

At noon the tired men went to eat their lunch and Boaz said to Ruth, 'Come along! You may eat with us.'

He gave Ruth delicious bread and sweet wine to satisfy her thirst. Later, when lunch was finished, Ruth went on looking for wheat. Boaz whispered to his servants, 'You must see to it that Ruth finds plenty of wheat. Drop a few extra ears here and there so that she can pick them up.'

Needless to say, Ruth found a lot of wheat that day. When evening came, she threshed the ears of grain and came home with a big bag of wheat kernels. Naomi was pleased and surprised. 'Where did you go to get all this?' she asked. Ruth told her everything that had happened.

The next day she went out again to the farm of Boaz and again the day after that. Ruth continued to gather wheat on Boaz' farm for as long as the men were harvesting. One day, after all the grain had been harvested, Boaz asked Ruth to marry him. So Ruth, who had been poor, became the wife of a wealthy farmer and some time later they had a little son. Naomi was delighted too: 'I have had great sadness in my life, but the Lord has made everything right again.'

S amuel

There once lived a woman called Hannah who was very unhappy because she thought she was unable to have children. To make matters worse, Elkanah's other wife, Peninnah teased her. 'The Lord has forgotten you and doesn't love you, that's why he doesn't give you a child!'

Whenever poor Hannah thought about this, tears would come to her eyes. Each year Hannah travelled to Jerusalem with her husband to visit the tabernacle, the house of God. There they would bring an offering to the Lord and pray. When they made this journey Hannah would receive a gift from her husband because he loved her very much. Although he wanted to make her happy she knew that only the Lord could make her really happy by answering her prayer.

One year when the time came for their visit to the tabernacle again, Peninnah teased her. Hannah was so sad she couldn't eat. 'I will tell the Lord all about my grief,' she said. When she came to the tabernacle she went inside and fell on her knees to pray. 'Dear God, please listen to me. Please don't forget me. Give me a child and I will take good care of him. I will tell him about you every day and I will do everything I can to help him to be your servant.'

Hannah prayed for a long time. She didn't want anyone to hear her so she whispered very softly. Nearby, at the door of the tabernacle, sat an old man wearing a beautiful blue robe. He was Eli, the high priest, and he was God's servant. He was head over all the other priests and looked after the tabernacle. Eli saw Hannah and thought, 'This woman is acting strangely. She just lies there on the ground with her lips moving, but I don't hear her voice. Perhaps she's drunk.' He walked over and gruffly asked her, 'Aren't you ashamed to come to the house of God when you're drunk?'

Hannah's eyes were full of tears as she looked at Eli. 'Oh no, I'm not drunk! But I have been very sad and have been telling the Lord all about my grief. I have been praying to God.'

Eli was sorry he had been angry with her and said, 'Go in peace. The Lord has heard your prayer and He will answer you.'

When Hannah returned to her husband her sadness had gone. She believed with all her heart that the Lord had heard her prayer. Indeed, the Lord did hear her prayer and he answered her with the very thing for which she had asked. A year later Hannah had a baby boy and she called him Samuel, which means: 'I have asked him of the Lord'. That year Hannah couldn't travel to the tabernacle with her husband because she had to stay at home to look after the baby.

A few years later she made the journey to the tabernacle and this time she brought Samuel along, dressed in a new white robe. He had grown into a fine sturdy boy who no longer needed his mother every day. Now he could become God's servant in the tabernacle. Together Samuel and Hannah went to speak to Eli, who was sitting by the door. He had grown much older and his hair was almost white. He didn't recognise Hannah, so she introduced herself: 'I am the woman who prayed here for a baby. This is the boy who was given to me by the Lord, and I promised him that he would be his servant. May he remain here in the tabernacle and help you?'

Eli was very glad to have Samuel to work in the temple for him. Hannah returned home alone but she was very happy that her son could remain in the house of God. Each year after this, she and her husband returned to the tabernacle to see Samuel, and to give him a new white robe to wear. Samuel thought it was wonderful to

be a servant of God and he did all kinds of tasks for Eli. He had a small room of his own near Eli's.

One night Samuel woke up with a start when he heard someone calling him. Samuel got up and went to the room where Eli was sleeping. 'Here I am,' he said, 'you called me, didn't you?'

But Eli answered, 'No, I didn't call you. Hurry back to bed!'

'Perhaps I was dreaming', thought Samuel and he went back to his room to sleep. But he was wakened again: 'Samuel, Samuel!' a voice called. This time Samuel was sure he wasn't mistaken, so he went back to Eli's room and said, 'Here I am. Now you called me.' But again Eli said, 'No, Samuel, I didn't call you. You must have dreamt that you heard some-body calling you. Just go back to bed and sleep.'

Poor Samuel couldn't understand it at all, but he obeyed Eli and went back to his room. He had just lain down when he heard the voice for the third time: 'Samuel, Samuel!' Back he went again to Eli: 'Surely you called me this time, didn't you?'

Then Eli realised whose voice it must be so he said, 'It was the Lord who called you. Go back and when you hear the voice again, say, "Speak Lord, your servant is listening.'

Samuel went back to his room where he lay quietly and waited. His heart thumped with reverence and fear. Did the Lord really want to speak to him? Again the voice of God spoke to him: 'Samuel, Samuel!' Softly Samuel replied, 'Speak, Lord, for your servant is listening.' Then the Lord spoke to Samuel. But the message from God was a very sad one. It was about the sons of Eli who did not love the Lord and who did not do what God had told them. God had warned them many times but they wouldn't listen. Now the Lord was going to punish them.

On hearing this, Samuel couldn't get back to sleep. Early in the morning as usual, he rose and went outside to open the doors of the tabernacle. Eli called him and asked, 'What did the Lord tell you last night?' Samuel had no choice but to tell him everything, even although the message was a very sad one for Eli and his family. Eli was stunned but simply said, 'He is the Lord. He must do what he thinks best.'

What God had said took place many years later when Samuel had grown up. War broke out and the men of Israel went to fight. Hophni and Phinehas, Eli's sons, were in the army and they were both killed on the same day. When their father heard the sad news he fell from his chair and also died.

Samuel was now the servant of God and he loved the Lord. Often he heard the voice of God speaking to him and he did everything the Lord told him to do.

D avid

Young David looked after his father's sheep. Early each morning he would go to the pen where the sheep sheltered for the night and each day he would take them to the fields. He was their shepherd and his job was to make sure they had enough to eat. When they were thirsty he would bring water for them to drink. He looked after them well. David also had to watch out for wild animals which might want to kill the sheep. When he saw one he would chase it away with stones from his sling or hit it with his shepherd's crook.

In the distance were the houses of Bethlehem where David's father and brothers lived. He was often alone in the fields with his sheep but he didn't mind at all as he was happy and content with life. To amuse himself he played on his harp and sang songs. The sound of his beautiful singing could be heard across the pastures.

David always felt as though there was somebody with him at all times. David loved the Lord and knew that God was everywhere. David thought, 'I'm taking care of the sheep and the Lord is taking care of me. The Lord is also a shepherd and I am one of his sheep.'

One day David was in the pasture with his flock when a lion came to kill a sheep. It crept through the bushes until suddenly it jumped on one of the sheep. When the lion pounced, David saw it and ran after it, not thinking about the danger to himself. When he caught up with the creature he struck out at it until it let go of the sheep. Then he killed the huge animal to make sure that it would not come back again to bother his sheep. Gently David took the sheep back to the flock.

One day a servant came to tell David he must come home at once, as someone had come to visit his father, Jesse. David was the youngest of eight sons who lived with his father. An old man with a long grey beard had come to the house. It was Samuel, who was now quite old, but still a good servant of God. The Lord

had told him to go to the home of Jesse as one of his sons would one day become king of Israel.

There already was a king, called Saul, but he wasn't a very good ruler. He had become disobedient and no longer wanted to listen to God. Samuel didn't know which of the sons was to be the one chosen to follow Saul, but he knew that God would point him out when all the boys came before him.

First came the eldest. He was a big strong man and Samuel thought, 'Probably it's this one! What a handsome king he would be!'

'No, Samuel,' said the Lord. 'It isn't this one. I don't look to see if my king will be big and strong. I look into his heart.'

Samuel shook his head and said, 'No, the Lord didn't choose this one.'

The second son came next and again Samuel shook his head.

One by one, the sons of Jesse came to Samuel, but each time the old servant of God said, 'No, the Lord didn't choose this one.'

Finally, Samuel asked, 'Are these all the sons you have, Jesse?'

'No, the youngest isn't here. He is with the sheep in the pasture.'

'Send for him at once,' said Samuel.

And that was why David had been called home. Samuel was waiting for him as his father led him inside. Then the Lord told Samuel, 'This is the one. David must be king over my people for he loves me with all his heart.'

Samuel rose and took a horn out of his pocket. It was filled with special oil for anointing. Pouring out the sweet-smelling oil on David's head, he said, 'The Lord says, "I anoint you, David, as King of Israel. In a few years you will become king, for your heart is full of love for God."'

What an amazing message this was. David, only a humble shepherd boy, being anointed king of all the people of Israel. David believed what the Lord had said for, when God makes a promise, he always keeps his word. David and his father were very happy indeed. They didn't talk about it, however, and they didn't tell anyone what had happened, in case King Saul got to know about it. Saul assumed that his son Jonathan would become king after him; certainly not a shepherd boy from Bethlehem!

avid goes to King Saul

King Saul was in his palace. Around him were many servants who did everything he commanded them to do. He was very rich and powerful and could have anything he asked for. Despite this, the king was both angry and sad. Samuel, the servant of God, had told him he wouldn't be king much longer because he hadn't loved the Lord, nor had he wanted to obey him.

'Another man will become king,' Samuel told him. 'A man the Lord himself has chosen, who loves the Lord with all his heart. He will be king in your place. He will live in your palace and sit on your throne.'

King Saul thought about this all the time and was annoyed about it.

'I want to be king for as long as I live' he thought, 'and after I die, my son Jonathan must rule in my place! I wish I knew who this other man is, for I would kill him if I could.'

The more he thought about it, the angrier he became and sometimes he was so furious the servants were afraid of him. They said to each other, 'Our king is sick. He is sick because God has left him and now his heart is dark and full of evil. I wish we could do something for him.'

Then they had an idea and went to see the king: 'Our lord, the King, we think it would help if somebody could come and play beautiful music for you. Perhaps it would be good for you and help you to get well again.'

'Alright, go and find a man who can do this,' said the king.

One of the servants said, 'I know a shepherd in Bethlehem. He is the son of Jesse and can play wonderful music on his harp.'
'Very well,' said the king. 'Send for him.'

One of the servants then went to Bethlehem and brought David to the palace. The king was having one of his wild fits of temper when David arrived. He was stomping through the rooms, shouting with grief and fury. As soon as David came in, he began to play one of his lovely songs. It was a beautiful tune and it was soothing to Saul's troubled mind. When he listened, his anger slowly melted away and he no longer shouted or stomped around. The soft music seemed to take all his troubles away.

David's music helped the king to become well again, and he was very pleased for him to stay on in the palace to play regularly for him. Saul grew very fond of David. Of course, Saul didn't know that the young man was the anointed king who would one day take his place.

avid & Goliath

War broke out in the land of Israel when they were attacked by the Philistines, who came to steal sheep and grain from the people. King Saul had called all his soldiers together to go out and defend the country. The Israelites were encamped close to the Philistines, who had a strong army. They had one man in particular who was stronger than all the others. He was a giant of a man called Goliath. He carried a large spear in his hand and a big sword hung from the belt around his waist. He had a coat made of bright shining armour and on his head he wore a helmet which glinted in the sunlight.

Every day the giant would taunt the Israelites. 'Who wants to fight? I am stronger than all of you put together! Come here, if any of you dare!' He laughed at them and he cursed. He teased Saul and his soldiers but, worst of all, he mocked God.

Each day he came out but nobody dared to fight him. Three of David's brothers, big strong soldiers, were there, but none of them came forward. They were all afraid of the giant and they trembled with fear when they saw him coming.

David, meanwhile, had gone back home to his father, because he didn't have to play for the king anymore. The king no longer had time to listen to music and David had returned home to look after the sheep. One evening, Jesse called David and said, 'David, I want you to go to your brothers who are with Saul's army. I want to know if they are alright and for you to take them some food.' David was pleased to have the opportunity to go and see something of the war.

Early the next morning he set out on the long journey until he came to where the Israelites were. No sooner had he arrived when Goliath came out again. He stood close to Saul's army, cursing and swearing, and mocking the soldiers. David was shocked when he heard it. The godless giant mocking the king was understandable, but to insult the Lord? David loved God with all his heart and this mockery made him very angry. Was there nobody to punish this wicked man?

DAVID AND GOLIATH

How well armed were they?

GOLIATH

Heavy bronze armour
Bronze helmet
Bronze leg protectors
Bronze javelin
Thick spear
Shield - carried by
a soldier

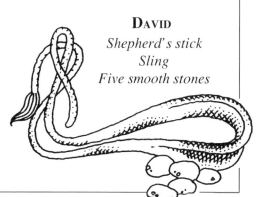

DAVID

Shepherd's stick
Sling
Five smooth stones

When he learned that no one was brave enough to fight Goliath in all of Saul's army, David said, 'I will fight him.'

'Do you really dare?' asked the soldiers. 'Do you really think you can fight this giant? If you do and win, you will receive the king's daughter for your wife and you will be given many fine presents. The king himself has said this.'

The soldiers brought David to the king. 'You are only a young shepherd boy,' said the king. 'How can you possibly want to fight with that giant? He is a big soldier, much bigger and stronger than you. No, I won't let you fight him.'

The Lord will help me, O King!' said David. 'This is why I can fight the giant. Once I fought with a lion while I was tending sheep and killed it, because the Lord helped me. I shall kill this wicked man who mocks God. The Lord will also help me to fight the giant.'

The king listened and agreed only when he realised that no one else would come forward to fight. He ordered a servant to bring David a coat made of iron. He put the coat on David and placed a shiny helmet on his head. Then Saul gave him his own big sword. He wanted to make a soldier out of David. But all these things were much too heavy for David. Quickly he took the armour off and gave the sword back to Saul.

Instead of weapons and armour, David took only his stick and his sling. Then he looked for five round smooth stones and put them in his pocket. In front of the two armies he went out to where the giant stood shouting and waving his arms. When Goliath saw him coming he laughed and cursed!

'Who is this?' he bellowed. 'What kind of a little fellow are you? You don't even have a sword, just a stick! Do you think I am a dog? Do you believe you can chase me away with your stick? Come here and I will beat you to death. The wild animals will eat you up when I'm finished with you.'

Goliath was furious and all those who heard him trembled with fear. David, however, was not frightened, for he knew the Lord was very close to him. 'You came to me with a sword and a spear,' said David, 'but I come to you because you have mocked my God. This is why I shall punish you!'

As he spoke he put a stone in his sling and, before the giant had time to hurl his spear, David swung the stone right at Goliath's forehead.

The stone flew straight through the air and when it struck the giant, he staggered and fell to the ground. It had hit him with such force that the one little stone from David's sling had killed him outright.

David walked over to where Goliath lay, took the giant's own sword and cut off his head. Never again would Goliath bother the people of Israel or mock the Lord!

The Philistines were shocked but

Saul's army was overjoyed. They shouted and cheered and were no longer afraid. Having seen how God had helped David, they came running and chased their enemies away.

The war was over and David was called before the king. 'Now you must always stay with me,' said King Saul. 'You are so strong and brave that you may now be in charge of some of my soldiers. When the enemies come again you must fight against them. Do not go back to your sheep for I need you here in the palace.'

King Saul's son, Jonathan, was also there and he liked David very much. He gave him presents, including his sword, his beautiful coat, his handsome belt and his bow and arrows.

'Let us always be friends,' said Jonathan.

David wanted very much to be Jonathan's friend, for he was very fond of him too. It had been a wonderful day, for David was now the friend of the king and his son.

But, above all, David knew that he was the Lord's friend and this was by far the most important of all.

D avid runs away from Saul

David was no longer a shepherd. Now he was a general and commander of many soldiers. When enemies came to Canaan he fought them. He fought well because the Lord was on his side. David now lived in a beautiful house close to the king's palace, and often he would eat with the king. The king's daughter became his wife and Prince Jonathan was his best friend. David had become an important man and the people who met him on the street bowed to him. 'David is strong and brave,' they said. 'He is the bravest and strongest of all!'

Even though David was enjoying many new and wonderful things, he did not become proud but kept on loving the Lord. 'I am not strong,' he thought. 'I cannot do very much alone, but when the Lord helps me I can do what he commands.'

There had been another war and once again David and his soldiers had been victorious in battle. Everyone in Canaan was celebrating and, when David came home with his soldiers, the people were waiting to greet him in the street. The women and the young girls walked in front of him in a long parade, and they were so glad the war was over that they made music and sang a special song: 'Saul has beaten a thousand enemies, but David has defeated ten thousand!'

When King Saul heard this he wasn't very happy about it, and became angry and jealous. Every day the words of the song kept going through his mind, and at night he couldn't sleep when he thought of David's popularity. Now he knew who the next king was going to be. He had seen it in the eyes of the people, for they loved David. He could also see it in David himself, for David loved the Lord with all his heart and he was very brave.

'The people want to put me off my throne,' thought Saul. 'They want to make David king.' Again he had one of his wild fits of temper, stomping his foot as he walked around the palace in a rage. His servants were very afraid of him.

David, however, was not afraid; rather he felt sorry for King Saul. One day he slipped quietly into the king's room to help him by playing some soothing music. He sat in a corner and played his most beautiful songs. This time, however, David was unable to help King Saul, who didn't get better, no matter how well David played.

Saul glared at David thinking, 'I will kill him! Then he will never become king!' Suddenly, he picked up his spear and threw it at David. He missed, but it slammed into the wall close to David's head. Terrified, David ran outside, thankful that the Lord had saved his life.

Clearly, David could no longer stay with the king. Even Jonathan agreed that David should go as far away as possible, where Saul couldn't find him. If he did find him surely he would try to kill David again.

Jonathan and David met outside the city in the fields where the two friends said goodbye. Perhaps they would never see each other again and they were very sad. They put their arms around each other and tears ran down their cheeks.

'Be patient, David,' said Jonathan. 'Some day you will become king in spite of my father. It is the Lord's will and I want it too. Will you be good to me and to my children when you become king?'

David hated to leave his friend and promised with all his heart to do as Jonathan had asked. He then fled from the city, away from the king, while Jonathan went back to the palace. David didn't know where to go for the king would try to catch him wherever he went. But he knew that the Lord would take care of him and this gave him peace and rest in his heart.

avid shows his love for the King

David could not return to his own house when he realised that Saul wanted to kill him. Neither could he return to his family home for the king was sure to look for him there. He moved from place to place: the desert, the woods or the mountains. Nowhere was safe, for the king was looking everywhere. King Saul hunted for David as a hunter hunts for a wild animal. There were times when he very nearly caught him but the Lord watched over David.

On one occasion, David was hiding deep in a cave in the side of a mountain so that the king would not be able to find him. Saul came looking around the area very close to the cave. David and his friends sat very quietly waiting for the king to pass by. The king was so close they didn't dare speak or even whisper! The soldiers approached the mouth of the cave unaware that David was inside.

When Saul saw the cave he said, 'That cave will be nice and cool. I'll lie down for a while and rest.' He stopped with his men and told them to rest in the shadow of the mountain while he went into the cave. When David and his men saw the king at the entrance, they held their breath. But Saul hadn't seen them hiding deep inside. It was lighter at the mouth of the cave where Saul lay fast asleep.

David and his men relaxed a little when they saw that Saul had fallen asleep. They laughed, 'Now our enemy is at our mercy. Go over to him, David, and punish him for his wickedness! Kill him! He will never again hunt for us and you will be our king.'

But David didn't want to become king in this way. 'No,' he said, 'I don't want to be a murderer. The Lord himself will punish King Saul.'

After a little while David got up from where he was hiding and crept over to the king. Taking his sword he cut off a small piece of Saul's coat and then tiptoed back to his friends. A little later, King Saul woke up and left the cave with his soldiers to continue to search for David.

They hadn't gone very far when David came out of hiding and called out: 'My lord the king!' Saul looked round and was amazed! Where could David have come from so quickly?

'My lord the king, why are you so angry with me?' asked David. 'I haven't done you wrong, have I? I could have killed you a short while ago but I didn't. I only cut off a small piece of your coat.' Then he held out the piece of cloth for Saul to look at.

King Saul was very ashamed of himself. Tears came to his eyes and he cried, 'David, my son, I have done you wrong, yet you have been kind to me. I hated you, but you have loved me in return.' Then Saul left with his soldiers for he no longer wanted to harm David.

T he spear and the water jug

Some time later, consumed with fear and jealousy, King Saul forgot how David had spared his life and began to hunt for him again.

One day when Saul had been searching for a long time without success it grew dark. He was exhausted and went to lie down in the tent which the soldiers had put up for him. Before he lay down he drove a spear into the ground, close to where he would lay his head and placed a jug of water nearby. Now the king felt safe. He had a spear near at hand to protect himself and water in case he became thirsty. Calling a couple of soldiers, he said, 'You must stay awake and keep guard. Wake me if something is wrong.' Then he lay down and fell fast asleep.

The soldiers who had come with Saul to look for David were also very tired, including the two he had asked to stand guard. Soon the entire camp was sleeping. Not a single man remained awake.

David and his friend Abishai had seen the king and his soldiers earlier in the evening when they had come close to where David was hiding. In the still of the night, the two men approached the king's camp, each with a sword in his hand. They crept past the sleeping guards right up to Saul's tent where he lay fast asleep. They could have done anything they pleased.

'Shall I kill him for you now?' asked Abishai. 'Surely he deserves it. Look how he has tried to kill you so many times.'

'Don't lay a finger on him!' whispered David. 'The Lord has forbidden it. God made him king and he will punish him if he so wishes.' But David took Saul's spear and water jug before the two of them vanished into the night, away from the camp.

In the morning, at sunrise, David climbed a mountain near Saul's camp. He shouted at the top of his voice to the soldiers below, waking them from their sleep. 'Why didn't you take better care of your king? He could have been dead by now. Look! I have his spear and his water jug. I could have harmed him, but I did not!'

King Saul also woke up. 'Is that you, David?' he asked.

'Yes, O King,' replied David. 'Why are you hunting for me all the time? I haven't done you any harm. Last night I stood next to you while you were sleeping but didn't put out my hand to harm you. Now do you believe I'm not your enemy?'

The king hung his head in shame. 'I'm sorry for what I have done. I am an evil man. Come with me to my palace and never again will I try to harm you.'

But David was afraid to trust Saul as he knew that the king would soon forget his promise. A soldier came to fetch the king's spear and water jug and took them back to Saul before he returned to his palace. David went to another land where the king couldn't find him, and they never saw each other again.

David becomes King

David lived far away from the palace of Saul. One day a messenger came to bring David sad news from the land of Canaan. The Philistines had come again to attack the people of Israel and had started a war. Saul and Prince Jonathan had taken all their soldiers to fight the Philistines, and both King Saul and Jonathan had been killed in the battle.

When he received the message, David knew that he no longer had to hide. No one would try to hunt for him any more because his enemy was dead.

Nevertheless, David was very sad to hear the news for he was very fond of the king, despite the fact that he had tried to kill him. Jonathan had been his close friend and the news of his death in particular grieved him very much.

David wept and could neither eat nor drink. When evening came he took his harp and sang a song in mourning for King Saul and Prince Jonathan.

David became king of Israel as foretold many years before, when Samuel visited his home in Bethlehem, while he was still a shepherd boy.

After he was crowned, he went to live at the palace in Jerusalem where he ruled over the whole kingdom. He was a man after God's own heart and David loved the Lord. Often he would remember how well the Lord had looked after him, had helped him time and time again, and had protected him from harm.

Sometimes he would pick up his harp to play and sing just as he had done many years before, when he was still a shepherd boy tending his father's sheep.

rince Absalom

King David had a son whose name was Absalom. He was a very handsome prince who was well-liked.

He thought to himself, 'If I were king, I would live in the palace and be ruler of the whole land. I would be the richest and most powerful person in Israel.'

But David, his father, was king, and he would have to die before Absalom could take over the throne. 'What a long time to have to wait,' he thought. 'I wish my father would get sick and die.'

The people were unaware of Absalom's thoughts for they could only see what the prince wanted them to see. He always seemed a kind person and the people admired him.

David remained very healthy and showed no signs of dying to allow his son to succeed him. The prince began to get impatient. He made up his mind to find a way to have David killed. With a few of his friends, he plotted against his father. 'Go ahead!' they told him. 'You can count on us to help you.'

Having made his plans he went to his father and asked, 'Father, may I go away for a few days? I want to bring an offering to the Lord in Hebron.'

King David was delighted and sent his son off to Hebron, a city not far from Jerusalem. As soon as the prince arrived in the city, he called all the people together to help him. They formed an army and Absalom led them back to Jerusalem to put his father off the throne. When they reached the palace, his servants blew their horns and shouted, 'Absalom is king in Hebron!'

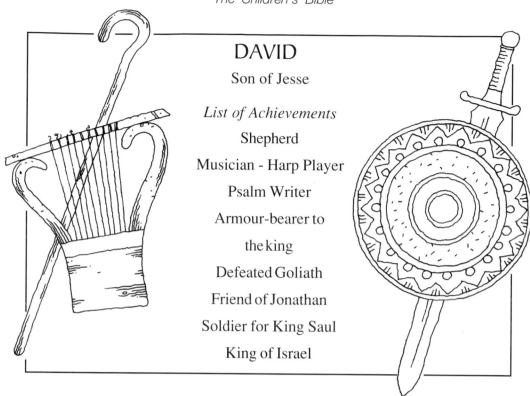

DAVID

Son of Jesse

List of Achievements

Shepherd

Musician - Harp Player

Psalm Writer

Armour-bearer to

the king

Defeated Goliath

Friend of Jonathan

Soldier for King Saul

King of Israel

David could not believe it when he heard of the plot against him. He couldn't understand why his own son would do such a thing and it grieved him greatly. 'Must I prepare my servants and my soldiers to fight against my own son? No, I will flee from him. The Lord sees and knows all things. If He wants me to be king he will bring me back to Jerusalem.'

With his head bowed in dismay David left the palace, crying as he walked through the streets. His friends and servants went with him, and many others who supported him followed.

They made their way from the city and walked towards the mountains, where they sought shelter from their enemies.

Absalom rode into Jerusalem with his army and took over the throne. Although he was now king he was still not content as he did not have all that

PSALMS

David wrote many of the
songs found in the book
of Psalms.
They were written to
express his feelings and
thoughts to God.
He praised God for all
the wonderful things
he had done.
He poured out all his
troubles to God, too,
knowing that God
was always listening.

The shortest chapter in the
Bible is Psalm 117.
The longest chapter is
Psalm 119.
One of the most famous of
the passages in the Bible
is Psalm 23 which begins:

The Lord is
my Shepherd

he wanted. Above all, he was afraid
that his father might return with an
army.

So he decided that he would look
for David and throw him into prison,
for only then would he feel really safe.

Absalom marched with his army
to the mountains where David and his
friends were in exile.

David had no alternative but to
send his army off to do battle with
Absalom's men. He couldn't bring
himself to go with them so he stayed
behind in the hills and waited for
news of the battle.

Despite his son's treachery, he
still loved him very much: 'I hope
nothing happens to Absalom. I hope
ho won't be killed. Please don't harm
my son,' he told his soldiers.

The two armies met in a big forest
and there they began to fight.
Absalom rode ahead of his soldiers
and fought with all his strength.

Although he had a good army,
David's men were much stronger,
because the Lord was helping them.

The battle was soon over and Absalom and the remains of his army ran away as fast as they could.

As Absalom fled through the forest his long hair got caught in the branches of a tree. The donkey he was riding kept on running but Absalom was left hanging . His beautiful long hair had been the cause of his undoing. David's men caught up with him and killed him as he hung helpless.

Meanwhile, David waited impatiently for news of the battle which he knew was going on somewhere in the forest. A man came running towards him and shouted, 'O King, we have won the battle!'

'And what about my son?' asked David, anxiously. But the soldier could give him no news. Then another came in to tell him of Absalom's death.

David wept openly and wrung his hands in grief for his dead son. 'Oh, my son Absalom! My son, my son! How I wish you were alive and I had died in your place!'

King David went back to Jerusalem to live in the palace. Once more he sat on his throne and everything was as it had been before. Every time David thought of Absalom he grew sad again for he loved his son, even although he had plotted against him.

King Solomon

When David died, his son Solomon became king of Israel. King Solomon wanted very much to be a good king and he worried about the task that lay ahead of him. As he was still a young man when he took over the throne, he was anxious that he would not be able to take care of his people.

'This work is much too hard for me,' thought Solomon. 'I am not nearly old enough, nor wise enough, to do the job properly.'

One day Solomon brought an offering to the Lord and then went to sleep. While he was sleeping God spoke to him. 'Solomon, I am going to give you a gift. You may choose whatever you would like to have. No matter what you ask for I will give it to you.'

'How wonderful,' thought Solomon. But what should he ask for? Should he ask the Lord to make him rich? Or should he ask to become great and powerful? Or to live for a very long time? But Solomon asked the Lord, 'Give me wisdom so that I may be a good king.'

'Very well, Solomon,' God said, 'I will make you wiser and more understanding than any man who has ever lived. Because you have chosen so well I will also make you rich, strong and powerful. If you always obey me, I will also give you a long life.'

When Solomon woke up, he was no longer afraid or restless but glad to be king, now that he knew that God would give him wisdom and strength to be the ruler of his people.

One day King Solomon was in his palace when two women came with a quarrel which they wanted the king to settle.

Each woman carried a baby. One of the babies was happy and lively but the other lay lifeless in the mother's arms.

'The living baby is mine,' one of the women said. 'No, it is mine,' protested the other.

King Solomon interrupted the argument and told the two women to tell him the whole story.

The first mother began, 'This woman and I live together in the same house. We each had a baby, but last night one of them died. It is her baby who died and the living child is mine.'

But the other argued, 'No, the living baby is mine, and the dead one is hers!'

They both knew the truth but did not confess, and it was hard to find out which baby belonged to whom. Solomon had to decide which of the women could keep the living baby, so he asked, 'Do both of you want the living child?'

'Yes, your majesty,' said the first. 'Certainly, sir,' said the other.

On hearing this King Solomon said something very unusual to the two women. 'Alright,' he said, 'we will cut the living baby in half. In this way you can have an equal share of the baby.'

Of course the king didn't mean what he had said but the women thought he was serious. Then he called a servant with a large sword and commanded, 'Cut the baby in half!'

Grabbing the child with one hand, the servant raised his sword. 'Oh no! Please don't!' cried one of the women. 'Don't hurt the baby. Give the baby to her, but please let it live!'

But the other woman didn't care. 'Go ahead,' she said, 'cut the baby in half, then neither of us will have anything!'

When he heard this, the king knew which of the women was the real mother. 'Give the child to the first

woman,' he said, 'for she loves it dearly and would rather lose it than have it dead!'

The child was given to the real mother and she went home happily with her baby. All the people said, 'How wise King Solomon is!'

Solomon was king for many years and he ruled his people well. He was known not only for his wealth but also for his wisdom and faithfulness to the Lord. As a mark of his love for God he built a beautiful temple, a place where people from all over the country would come to worship and present their offerings.

lijah and King Ahab

The people of Israel were unhappy. A wicked king called Ahab and his wife Jezebel had taken over the throne and they did not rule the country well.

King Ahab and Queen Jezebel said, 'We don't love the Lord God. We want to worship another god.' Then they made themselves an idol called Baal and knelt down to pray before it as their priests brought offerings. They told the Israelites, 'You must also pray to Baal. Forget about the God of your forefathers!'

Because the king had commanded it, the people felt that they should obey, and believed that it must be alright to do so. By bowing to this idol they were disobeying the word of the Lord. Because of their disobedience, things began to go terribly wrong.

One day the king was sitting on his throne when suddenly the door opened and a strange looking man came in. He appeared to be very poor because he wore a long grey coat with a leather belt around his waist, but he wasn't in the least ashamed to come in to the palace dressed like that. To the king's astonishment, he spoke directly to him with a stern look in his eyes.

'I am Elijah, the servant of God. The Lord has sent me to bring you punishment for your sins. The punishment will be this: there will be no more rain in the country, nor will there be any dew at night until I say so!'

Having passed on the message, Elijah turned and walked out of the palace as quickly as he had come in. Everyone was stunned and for a moment no one said a word. The king and his servants were startled at first by the words spoken by the stranger, but then they began to laugh. 'What a funny man!' they said. 'He thinks he can hold back the clouds and the rain!'

But many days and weeks passed without rain. Each day the sun burned like a huge fire in the sky and everything on the earth dried up. The grass withered, the flowers faded and the leaves fell from the trees to blow away in the scorching breeze. The people needed wheat to make bread, but the crops had dried up in the drought and they had nothing to eat. Soon there was famine everywhere, but still the rain didn't come.

When the king saw that Elijah had spoken the truth he became afraid. 'It's Elijah's fault!' he cried. 'He's the one who's caused this. Look everywhere and bring him to me.'

While the people of Israel were suffering from thirst and hunger, Elijah was hiding beside a small river in the mountains. The Lord had shown him where to go to keep away from the soldiers of King Ahab. Elijah slept in a cave near the stream and the Lord took good care of him. He did not go hungry, for each morning and evening God sent ravens to bring him food. They dropped pieces of bread and meat at the entrance to the cave so that he could have food every day.

The people of Israel suffered greatly from hunger and thirst because they had forgotten God; but Elijah had enough to eat and drink because he had remained a faithful servant of the Lord.

lijah and the widow

For a long time Elijah remained in the cave in the mountains. But a time came when even the stream began to dry up because there was no rain and Elijah had to move on. The Lord told Elijah to travel to another country, where he would meet a woman who would help him.

After many days journey, Elijah reached the country the Lord had told him about. He was thirsty and hungry after the long trek, when he met a woman who was gathering firewood. 'Would you bring me some water to drink? I'm terribly thirsty,' he asked the woman. When she kindly brought him something to drink, Elijah said, 'And would you also give me a little bread to eat as I am very hungry?'

She shook her head when Elijah asked her for bread, 'No sir, I cannot, for I have no more bread in the house. I have a bowl with only a handful of flour and a jar with just a few drops of oil and this is all I have. I have just gathered a few sticks so that I can bake just one more roll for my little boy and myself then that will be the end of it.'

She believed that she and her son were about to die. To her surprise, Elijah said, 'Go home and bake, then come and bring it to me. Then you will be able to bake more for your son and yourself. There will be plenty, for the Lord has told me that the flour in the bowl will not be used up, nor will the oil in your bottle run out. The three of us will eat rolls made of these things until the rains come again and there is enough food to eat.'

These were amazing words but the woman believed them! Taking her armful of sticks home she made a fire in her open stove and with the remaining flour and oil she baked as her son watched. To the mother's great surprise, there was still flour in the bowl and oil in the jug. She almost wept with joy, she was so happy that the Lord had performed such a great miracle.

The woman kept baking, first for Elijah and then for herself and her son. The Lord had kept his word and was taking care of them.

Some time later, while Elijah was still with the woman and her boy, a very sad thing happened. The boy became ill. His breathing became slower and slower until finally it stopped altogether.

The mother was extremely upset by her boy's death and she cried for a very long time. She sat with him in her arms and called his name over and over, but it was no use. Her son was dead and would soon have to be buried.

Elijah felt sorry for the mother and asked her to give him the child. Taking the dead boy from her lap, he laid him on the bed in his room. Then he knelt beside him. 'If the Lord has allowed the boy to die, then surely he can bring him back to life.' He then began to pray, 'Lord, my God, let this child live!'

The Lord heard the prayers of his servant and the boy began to breathe again. He opened his eyes and lifted his head. Overjoyed, Elijah took him by the arms and brought him back to his mother. She did not know what to say. How could this be? The boy hugged his mother and she wept openly with joy. 'Now I know that you're a great prophet and a true servant of the Lord!' she said to Elijah.

 lijah and the Priests of Baal

Elijah stayed at the widow's house for a long time and still not a drop of rain fell in Israel. This was the punishment given to King Ahab and the disobedient people of Israel. For more than three years almost nothing grew on the land. Finally the punishment ended.

'Go to King Ahab,' the Lord told Elijah. 'I am going to send rain again.' Elijah did as he was told and went to the king. The king was very angry when he saw Elijah.

'So there you are!' he shouted. 'You're the one who's given us all this trouble and caused this drought and famine.'

'No!' replied Elijah. 'It wasn't I who troubled Israel, but you! You are the man who forgot the Lord and prayed to the idol Baal. Now listen, and I will tell you what you must do. Call the people together along with the priests of Baal and bring them to a high mountain.'

King Ahab was very afraid of Elijah and he didn't dare disobey him, so he gathered the people and the priests by the high mountain.

'Now I will show you that the Lord is our God!' Elijah told the people. 'You must never forget him again. The Lord can do all things and Baal can do nothing. Now listen, for this is what we shall do. The priests of Baal will prepare an offering and I will do the same. We will not, however, burn our offerings. First, the priests of Baal will pray to their God to send fire for their offering. Then I will pray to the Lord to send fire for my offering. The God who sends the fire from heaven will be our God!'

The people agreed. The priests of Baal began their work by piling stones to make an altar. Then they placed wood on the stones and meat on top of the wood. This was to be their offering. Then they began to pray, calling, 'Baal, O Baal, hear us! Give us fire, O Baal! O Baal, answer us!'
But no fire came to burn their offering. Louder and louder they cried, calling, 'Baal, O Baal, answer us!' Still no fire. They grew tired, but still they kept on calling until they were hoarse with all the praying. But Baal did not answer and no fire came down.

Finally, Elijah called to his people, saying, 'Now come near to me and I will begin.' He made an altar also and placed wood on top of the stones. On the wood he placed the meat and then dug a ditch around the pile of stones before he poured water over the entire offering. He made everything soaking wet and water filled the ditch as well.

Elijah then knelt down near the altar and everyone was quiet. It was time for him to pray, but he didn't shout as the priests of Baal had done for he knew the Lord would hear him. Quietly and reverently he prayed, 'Lord God of Abraham,

Isaac and Jacob, let the people see that you alone are their God and that I am
your servant. O Lord, answer me that they may never again forget you.'

That was all Elijah needed to say. Fire fell from heaven on to the offering and
burned it with huge blazing flames. The people ran away from the heat, and
the water in the ditch sizzled in the fury of the fire! Seeing this, the people fell
on their knees and called out, 'The Lord is our God! The Lord is our God!' They
realised how blind and foolish they had been. Baal could do nothing but the Lord
could do great things. How could they ever have forgotten the God of their
forefathers?

Later, when the people had all left to return to their homes, Elijah remained
alone on the mountain. Once again he prayed to the Lord but this time he didn't
ask for fire but for rain. That same evening big clouds came drifting over the
land and the rain poured down. The grass became green again and the flowers
bloomed once more. The trees put forth new leaves and the wheat grew. As
soon as it had ripened the people gathered the harvest.

aaman and Elisha

There was a little girl who lived with her father and mother in the beautiful land of Canaan. A war had broken out and foreign soldiers invaded the country. They stole and robbed and even took back slaves with them to their own land. One of the slaves was the little girl who became a servant to a great general in the army.

The general's name was Naaman. He accepted the girl and gave her to his wife to become her maid. The poor girl was far from home and away from her parents, but she soon found out that Naaman and his wife were good people and she grew quite fond of them. Naaman was a very rich man with servants and many beautiful things. He could have anything he wanted.

Even though he had all these things he was a very sad man for he had a terrible disease. There were large white swollen sores on his face, hands and feet. Naaman had leprosy and no-one could cure him. He grew worse and worse with each passing week and his friends were afraid that he would soon die.

One day the little servant girl spoke to her mistress, Namaan's wife. 'If the master were in my country where my father and mother live, he could be cured of his leprosy. There is a prophet in Canaan whose name is Elisha, and he is a servant of God.'

After she had listened to what the little girl had to say, Naaman's wife told her husband about Elisha. 'Is it really possible for me to get well again?' Naaman wondered. He decided to go to the land of Canaan immediately, so he gathered his servants and prepared for the journey.

He rode in a beautiful carriage and took expensive presents of gold and silver to give to Elisha if he were able to make him well again. It was a long journey but finally Naaman came to a river called Jordan. He and his servants crossed into the land of Canaan and they soon arrived at the house of Elisha.

'Elisha will be very happy to have such a rich man coming to him,' thought Naaman. 'He will probably run to the door when he sees me and bow before me. Maybe he will pray with me and gently touch the swellings on my body to cure me of the leprosy.'

But Elisha didn't come out of the house at all. He sent a servant out to speak to Naaman: 'You must go to the river Jordan and wash yourself seven times. When you have done that you will be healed.' Then the door closed again and Naaman was left standing outside, angry and disappointed.

'Did I come all this way just to be told to wash myself in the river Jordan?' he said. 'This won't make me well, for I've washed myself many times and it has never made any difference at all! Come along, let's go back to my own country where there are more pleasant rivers to bathe in, for I fear I will keep this disease until the day I die.'

Namaan turned to go back home with his servants, who were also very disappointed at what had happened. They wanted to see their master healed so they asked him, 'Why are you so angry? Why don't you believe the prophet? You could at least try it, couldn't you? Wash yourself in the river seven times and perhaps you will be cured.'

They managed to persuade Naaman to do what Elisha had asked him to do. It certainly wouldn't hurt him to try and perhaps it would work. When he came to the banks of the Jordan, Naaman took off his fine clothes, and limped down to the water's edge on his sore feet.

The first, second and third times he washed himself it made no difference at all. But he did not give up. Four, five, six times he washed. When he came up out of the water the seventh time he jumped and danced for joy, for the swellings had disappeared! His hands and feet were no longer deformed and he felt well again. It was a miracle, and Naaman marvelled that Elisha was such an amazing man with such wonderful powers.

But it wasn't Elisha who had cured the leprosy. He was only the servant of God who had prayed for Naaman to be made well again. Naaman wanted to go at once to thank Elisha and to offer him some of the expensive gifts he had brought for him. 'Pick out whatever you'd like to have,' he said. 'Take whatever you want of the gold, silver or the fine clothes.'

But Elisha shook his head and said, 'I want nothing at all. I didn't make you well and you do not need to thank me. You must thank the Lord, for it was he who healed you.'

'Then I will bring the Lord an offering,' said Naaman. 'I want to love him forever and I will always remember him.'

The beautiful presents were then carefully put back into the carriage and Elisha went back into his house as Naaman left to return to his own country. As the coach drove off into the distance, Gehazi, Elisha's servant stood watching, thinking about all the expensive gifts. He was surprised that his master had turned down the offer of such wealth. If Naaman had asked him, he wouldn't have refused the chance to become a rich man.

As he stood watching the coach disappear into the distance with all the fine gifts, Gehazi decided to run after it. He caught up with Naaman and his servants, 'Stop! Wait a minute!'

When Naaman heard the servant calling, he stopped the coach and jumped down. 'What's the matter?' he asked. 'Is something wrong?'

'Sir,' answered Gehazi, 'Elisha would like a gift after all! He would like a bag full of silver and two of those nice coats. He has just received two visitors and he'd like to give them something.'

'That's quite alright,' said Naaman. Then he gave Gehazi two bags of silver and two of the fine coats.

Gehazi was very pleased with himself. Now he was rich and could buy anything he wanted. But first he had to hide the presents because he didn't want Elisha to know what he had done. Then he went home and behaved as if nothing had happened.

'Where have you been, Gehazi?' asked Elisha.

'I didn't go anywhere,' he replied, afraid to tell the truth.

Elisha shook his head and said, 'Gehazi, you thought no one saw you. The Lord saw what you did. Do you really believe that money and fine clothes can make you happy? Because of what you have done, you will become very unhappy, for the leprosy which Naaman once had will now afflict you.

Gehazi's face, hands and feet began to swell up and the leprosy spread all over his body. Soon he became very ill. Gehazi had the fine gifts and was wealthy, but because he had forgotten God he would not be able to enjoy them.

Naaman put his trust in God and lived to enjoy life to the full. He would never again forget the Lord.

J onah

Jonah was a servant of God who preached to the people of Israel about how they should live to please the Lord. One day God said to him, 'Jonah, I want you to go on a journey to the city of Nineveh. The people there are doing many wrong things and you must tell them that I have seen it all. You must warn them that I shall punish them unless they mend their ways.'

'Let them sin and be punished,' thought Jonah. 'They are the enemies of my people and I don't want to go to deliver a message to them and save them.' So he decided that he would not go to Nineveh with the warning from God. Instead, he went in the opposite direction. God had told him to go east but Jonah went west to get as far away from the place as possible.

'I will run far away where God cannot find me. Then I won't have to go to Nineveh.'

Jonah walked until he reached the sea. There he found a ship which was just getting ready to set sail. 'I'll go on board,' thought Jonah. 'It will take me still further away and God will never be able to find me.'

The captain didn't mind if Jonah sailed with his ship, as long as he paid his fare like any other passenger. It was a beautiful day when they left port. The sky was blue and the sun shone brightly.

However, Jonah was not up on deck with the others. He was tired from so much walking and had gone below to the bottom of the ship where he fell fast asleep. He was trying to hide from God but the Lord saw Jonah in the hold of the ship and had plans for him.

They were not very far out at sea when black storm clouds gathered, hiding the sun. Soon a wind blew up and the waves got higher and began to buffet against the side of the ship.

The storm got steadily worse and the ship was in danger of sinking. The captain and his crew were hardy sailors but they had never experienced a storm like this before. They were terrified. But Jonah slept down below, totally unaware of the commotion on deck.

The captain went to him and shook him, saying, 'How can you sleep like this? Wake up and help us. Pray to your God to save us from the storm, or else we will all drown!'

Jonah went up on deck, where he saw the huge waves and the big black clouds. He heard the howling of the wind and knew the Lord had found him. 'It is my fault that the storm has come,' he said. 'The Lord has sent it because I have done wrong. I was told to go to the east, but I went to the west. I have been disobedient and I tried to run away from God, but it was foolish. Nobody can hide from God! Take me and throw me into the sea. This will be my punishment and I have deserved it. The sea will be quiet again after I am gone, for the Lord will call back the storm.'

But the crew didn't want to throw Jonah overboard. Instead they sailed on, trying to get back to shore. The wind blew harder and harder, and the sea roared higher and stronger until the waves almost engulfed the ship. No matter how hard the sailors tried to bring the ship back to shore, they couldn't. Having tried everything else, they finally took Jonah and threw him into the sea.

No sooner was Jonah gone from the ship when the wind dropped and the sea became calm. When the men saw what had happened they said, 'How powerful God is! Even the wind and the sea obey him.' They were overawed, and grateful that he hadn't allowed the storm to sink their ship.

Jonah was sure that he was going to drown but God had other plans for him. God sent a large fish to swallow him. It wasn't very pleasant inside the stomach of the fish but at least he was alive. Inside the fish he had time to think about what he had done. He knew that he had not been a faithful servant of the Lord.

'God sees me and can hear me I am sure. Now, I will promise always to obey the Lord.'

God sent the fish to the shore where it spat Jonah out of its stomach and on to a beach in his own country. Again the Lord told Jonah, 'You must go to the city of Nineveh. When you get there I will tell you what to say.'

This time Jonah didn't even think of refusing and began to travel in the right direction. When he reached the city of Nineveh after a long journey, God told him to tell the inhabitants that in forty days the whole city would be destroyed.

'This is a fine message,' thought Jonah. 'The city will be destroyed. It is just what those wicked people deserve for they are my enemies and the enemies of Israel.' He walked through the streets of the city, calling out everywhere, 'In forty days Nineveh will be destroyed!'

Everyone, from the king in his palace, to the men and women in the streets and market places, shook with fear. They knew that they had done many wrong things and deserved to be punished.

The king told his subjects, 'We must all pray and ask the Lord to forgive us and spare us. We must repent of our sins and do no more evil.'

That was exactly what they did. The whole population, men, women and children began to pray to the Lord for mercy. The Lord heard their prayers and saw that they were really trying to repent, so he did not punish Nineveh.

During this time, Jonah sat on a hillside not far from the city. The people of Nineveh were his enemies and he wanted very much to see their city in ruins. He had no pity on them at all. Jonah waited and waited but, to his surprise, nothing happened. He was disappointed and angry that he had come all this way to see his enemies punished, only to have God forgive them and save the city. God wanted to take the hatred from Jonah's heart and so he gave him a sign.

A tree began to grow next to Jonah while he sat on the hill above the city. It grew quickly until it became big enough for him to go under its branches to shade himself from the scorching sun. Jonah was pleased that God had sent him the tree to protect him from the heat.

But the next morning, the tree died and the leaves withered and fell to the ground. God had sent a worm to eat through the roots so that it could not get water to grow. Jonah could not find a place to shade from the sun as it beat down on his head and he became angry with God for allowing this to happen to the tree.

'Jonah,' God said, 'You feel sorry for a tree! May I not have pity on all those men, women and children in Nineveh?'

Jonah was ashamed of himself and realised how wise, kind and merciful God was to save the people of Nineveh.

T he good King Hezekiah

Once there lived a young prince who loved the Lord. His name was Hezekiah. After his father died, Hezekiah became king of Israel. The people of Israel, however, had forgotten the Lord and had begun to worship idols. They no longer thought about God, nor visited the beautiful temple in Jerusalem which Solomon had built as a house for the Lord. They had even nailed up the temple doors so that no one could get in.

Every year their enemies came to attack them. This was the punishment they had to suffer for having forgotten the Lord. But when Hezekiah became king, he knew that his people were doing wrong. 'We can't go on like this,' he said to the people. 'We must serve the Lord again and truly be the people of God. I will do all in my power to make this happen.'

Hezekiah immediately went to work and had all the idols smashed to pieces. He sent men to re-open the doors to the great temple in Jerusalem and had the house of the Lord cleaned from top to bottom. Then he sent his servants through the land, calling all the people to Jerusalem. 'Now we will all bring offerings,' he said. 'We will go to the house of God and ask the Lord to forgive us our sins.'

Hezekiah was a strict king but a good one, and the people did as they were told. When they brought their offerings to the Lord they also celebrated with a huge feast. The days which followed were wonderful for the people of Israel. They now wanted to love God and in doing so they became strong and happy. They were truly God's people again.

Hezekiah went out with his army and attacked his enemies, so that they wouldn't come back to bother the Israelites. But Hezekiah wasn't satisfied. There was so much that he wanted to do to ensure that the nation became stronger, and that the people would love the Lord even more.

Suddenly, in the middle of all his work, Hezekiah became very ill. He grew worse and worse and none of his doctors could find a cure. Hezekiah became very sad for he wanted to be well enough to continue the work he had started. When he was thinking about these things the door to his room opened. Isaiah, the prophet, a servant of the Lord, came in to deliver a message from God to the king. But it was a very sad one.

'My king, the Lord has said that the time has come for you to say good-bye to your family and friends for soon you will die.'

Hezekiah wasn't afraid to die for he dearly loved God and knew he would go to be with him. Nevertheless it saddened him very much because he still had many things to do for his people. His great work for God wasn't finished yet.

After Isaiah left, Hezekiah turned his face to the wall and sobbed out his terrible grief. 'O Lord,' he cried, 'let me live just a little longer! Allow me to continue working for my people. I do so want to make them happier and stronger.'

A little while later the door opened and in came Isaiah again. This time he brought a happy message for the king. 'The Lord says, "I have heard your prayer and I have seen your tears. I will make you well, and you will live for another fifteen years. I will also help you overcome your enemies."'

This news was so wonderful that Hezekiah could hardly believe his ears. As God had promised, three days later the king was well again and could go outside for the first time in many weeks. The first place he visited was the house of God. The Lord had done a wonderful thing for King Hezekiah and now he wanted to thank God.

A few years later the Lord showed Hezekiah an even greater wonder. A foreign king had come with a large army to attack Jerusalem. They wanted to destroy the city, to rob and set fire to all the houses, and then capture King Hezekiah.

Around Jerusalem was a high wall which the enemy soldiers would have to climb before they could capture the city. The Israelites closed and bolted the doors as soon as they saw the enemy coming. The army camped around the walls and laid siege to the city so that no one could get in or out. There they waited for a long time, making sure that no food could be brought into the city.

It was a very desperate time for the people of Jerusalem. They still had a little food but, if the soldiers didn't leave soon, there would be nothing left to eat and they would have to open the gates. Everyone, including the king, feared for their lives.

'There is someone who can help us,' said Hezekiah and he went to the temple where he prayed to the Lord. 'O Lord, please help us and save Jerusalem from destruction!'

A short time after he had prayed, Isaiah came to the king and said, 'Don't be afraid for the Lord has said that he will help you. Your enemies will not get into Jerusalem.'

A little later, a letter came from the enemy king making fun of the Lord. In it he wrote, 'Do not believe that your God will help you. He is unable to save you! Don't let God fool you any longer, for I am much stronger than He is!'

Hezekiah decided to take the letter to the temple, where he opened it before the Lord for he knew that only God could answer it. God did just that and, when night fell, an angel came down from heaven and passed through the enemy camp like a plague. The angel brought God's answer to the letter by bringing a terrible punishment.

In the morning more than a hundred thousand soldiers lay dead. The ones who were left were so terrified that they ran straight back to their own country. Never again would they dare to come back to Jerusalem, for they were very afraid of the God of Hezekiah.

No other enemies attacked Israel while Hezekiah was alive and the people of Israel lived happily and in peace.

he Israelites in Babylon

After King Hezekiah died everything went wrong again in Israel. Other kings came to the throne who didn't love the Lord. They chose instead to worship idols, as many had done before them. The people of Israel did as their rulers said, forgetting about the God of their forefathers. The Lord had been patient with his people for a long time, and he had often warned them through the prophets that they would be punished if they did not heed his words.

Foreign armies invaded Israel and destroyed the city of Jerusalem. They burned Solomon's beautiful temple and took the people away as prisoners to Babylon, the enemy's homeland. The Israelites became slaves of the Babylonians and remained captive there for a very long time until the Lord was no longer angry with them.

The king of Babylon was called Nebuchadnezzar, and he ruled over half the world. He lived in a magnificent palace with many servants. The king insisted that his servants should be important people held captive from countries they had conquered. Among the servants of king Nebuchadnezzar were four young men taken from Israel; one of them was called Daniel.

It was both difficult and dangerous to be a servant of King Nebuchadnezzar, for he was a very proud and severe ruler. If one of the king's servants displeased him, he would simply have his head cut off. In Babylon the king was very powerful indeed and his word was law. Nevertheless, Daniel and his three friends were not afraid, because they loved the Lord and were confident that he would protect them from harm.

One night king Nebuchadnezzar had a strange dream. It bothered him so much that he woke up with a start, his heart thumping with fear. It disturbed him and he couldn't get back to sleep again. What was worse, he was unable to remember what the dream had been about. But it had been so vivid at the time that he believed there must be some hidden meaning.

King Nebuchadnezzar had many wise and learned men whom he consulted when he needed guidance or had to solve a problem. When he got up the next morning he sent for them and told them about his strange experience in the middle of the night.

'I have had a dream and I must know what it means.'

The wise men bowed deeply before the king and answered, 'Your majesty, tell us your dream and we will explain what it means.'

'No,' said the king, 'You are the wise men in my kingdom. You tell me what the dream was and I will reward you with gold. However, if you are not able to tell me what I dreamt, I will have you put to death.'

The wise men were terribly afraid and protested, 'Your majesty, no one in the world can tell you what your dream means if you cannot remember it yourself.

The king was furious with them. 'You are liars, all of you!' he shouted. 'You say you know everything that we need to know, but you know nothing at all!'

Then he called his soldiers and ordered them to execute all the wise men in Babylon who were unable to tell him about his dream. When they came to the house of Daniel he asked to be taken immediately to King Nebuchadnezzar. 'Wait until tomorrow, your majesty, and I shall be able to tell you what you dreamt during the night,' he said confidently.

The king agreed to wait and Daniel then went to speak to his friends. 'There's only one who knows what the king has dreamt, ' he said to them, 'God himself and we must ask him to tell us.'

They prayed to the Lord together and during the night Daniel had the same dream the king had, but this time God gave him the meaning of it. Daniel was very pleased and he thanked God for helping him. Then he quickly returned to the palace to speak to King Nebuchadnezzar.

'Can you really tell me what I dreamt?' asked the king.

'No!' replied Daniel. 'I am not able to do this, for no man can do such a thing, but there is a God in heaven who knows all things. He told me about your dream.'

Then Daniel went on to tell the king about his dream. 'You saw a very great statue,' he said, 'so large that you were amazed by it. The head of the statue was gold and the breast silver. The stomach was made of copper and the legs of iron. The feet were made of iron and clay. Near the statue was a mountain and a stone came rolling down the side of it. The stone hit the feet of the statue and the statue fell. The stone smashed the statue into pieces so small that there was nothing left of it. The stone itself, however, grew bigger and bigger until it was as big as the whole world.

'This was your dream, your majesty, and there is a hidden meaning to it: The stone was stronger than the entire statue in the same way that God is stronger than all the kingdoms of the world. That is what it means!'

King Nebuchadnezzar's eyes were wide with amazement, for now he could remember it all. This was exactly what he had dreamt and he said, 'Daniel, what a mighty God you have!'

He gave Daniel all kinds of expensive and beautiful gifts and gave him an important job to do in the country. Daniel's three friends were also honoured by the king.

T rial by fire

Daniel's three brave friends served the king well. They knew how severe he could be with people, but they were confident that the Lord would always protect them.

Some time after the incident with the dream, King Nebuchadnezzar had a large statue built, a golden image which everyone would have to bow to, not unlike the one that he had seen in his dream. Nearby he had a large furnace constructed which was fired to a great heat. He called his vast army of servants, about a thousand of them, and told them what was soon to happen. 'Attention, all of you. In a short time you will hear music. When it starts to play you must all fall down in front of this great idol and pray to it. If you refuse you will be thrown into the furnace I have made.'

It was very quiet; all you could hear was the roar of the huge fire. Great black clouds of smoke rose to the sky. Everyone was very afraid and, as soon as the music started to play, they all fell on their knees to pray to the image. All, that is, except the three friends of Daniel. Shadrach, Meshach and Abednego remained standing and refused to bow before the idol. They were sent to the king immediately.

'Did you do that on purpose?' he asked. 'I will give you one more chance. If you don't kneel this time, I shall have you thrown into the furnace. Who will help you then?' But the men were not afraid and said, 'Your majesty, we cannot kneel before an image, for our God has forbidden us to do such a thing. If you have us thrown into the fire God will be able to help us.'

The king flew into a rage at their disobedience and ordered the fire to be made seven times hotter than normal. Then he called his strongest soldiers and told them to throw the three men into the fire. The heat was so great that even the soldiers who approached the furnace with the men collapsed and died. The king watched the scene intensely as the three men were thrown into the fire. Suddenly his eyes widened. Shielding himself from the heat he gazed into the depth of the furnace and exclaimed loudly, 'Didn't we throw three men into the fire?'

'Yes three,' replied his servants.

'But now there are four,' continued the king. 'Look for yourselves and notice, the fourth one doesn't look like a man, he looks like a god!'

Moving as close as he dared to the furnace, he shouted to the men who seemed to be walking around unharmed despite the heat: 'If you are alive, come out!' The three friends walked out of the furnace as if nothing had happened. Not a single hair on their heads had been burned and their clothes didn't even smell of fire. The three friends had trusted in God and he had protected them from danger. Nebuchadnezzar learned that there was one much more powerful than he was, the God of the Israelites.

aniel in the Lion's Den

Daniel had become an old man. His hair and beard had turned grey but he still lived in Babylon, where he remained an important servant of the king. King Nebuchadnezzar had died many years before and now there was another king whose name was Darius.

King Darius respected Daniel greatly as one of his most faithful servants. He gave him important work to do and made him governor of the kingdom. When some of the other servants heard of this they were jealous of Daniel and plotted against him.

'We don't want this foreigner to rule over us. Let us watch Daniel very carefully to see if he does anything wrong. Then we can tell the king about it and have him removed.' They secretly spied on Daniel every day, to see if he did anything against the laws of the king. But they could find no fault with Daniel, because he worked hard as an obedient servant. Busy as he was, however, he always found time to pray to the Lord. This he did three times a day, kneeling unashamedly in his room in front of an open window.

Far away lay Jerusalem, where the beautiful temple had once stood. Some day the people of Israel would return to their land and another temple would be built. This was Daniel's hope and prayer as he looked out of his window in the direction of Jerusalem. 'Lord, let your people be free again and allow them to go back to their own country to worship you in your holy temple.'

The other servants noticed the fact that Daniel prayed every day. This gave them an idea which they knew would upset him, a plan which would lead to his downfall as the king's favourite servant.

They went to the king and bowed before him. 'Your majesty, we have thought of a good way to ensure that everyone respects only you as king of this land. You must order all the people to ask nothing from anyone for a whole month.

They must ask nothing from God or man but only from you as the mighty king of Babylon.'

King Darius liked the idea and agreed to make it law. 'Anyone who doesn't obey shall be punished most severely and thrown into the den of lions.'

The law was decreed thoughout the whole of Babylon. No one was to pray to any god but had to bow only to King Darius. Everyone, including Daniel, soon heard about the order and he knew very well who had influenced the king. It would be very hard for those who worshipped the God of Israel. But Daniel loved the Lord and, although he was the king's most respected servant, he continued to pray to God three times a day.

In order to trap Daniel, his enemies had spies positioned under his window. As soon as they saw him pray as usual, they quickly went to the king 'Your majesty, didn't you say that no one should pray to any god for an entire month?'

'Yes,' answered the king, 'indeed I did.'

'And anyone who disobeyed must be thrown into the lions' den?' the men added.

'Yes,' said the king, 'that is what I ordered.'

'Well, sir,' they continued, 'your servant Daniel must be thrown to the lions, for he has disobeyed you. He prays to his God three times a day.

We have proof that he does this.' The king was shocked and dismayed. He was now aware how jealous the other servants were of Daniel. 'Not Daniel,' he cried. 'No, not Daniel!'

But the men said, 'You said so yourself, O king, and now you must do it, for your word is law!'

A decree of the king could not be broken in Babylon. Whatever the king said, had to be done. No matter how much the king wanted to help Daniel, he could not change the law even for his most respected servant.

When evening came, Daniel was brought to the lions' den. The king was upset that he had been tricked. 'Daniel, I cannot do anything for you but I hope the Lord will help you.' Then Daniel was thrown to the lions.

That night King Darius could not sleep as he thought of Daniel. In his heart he hoped that Daniel's God would save him. First thing in the morning Darius made straight for the lions' den to find out if Daniel was still alive. He shouted in a loud voice, 'Daniel! Daniel!'

To his amazement, a voice came back, 'I am well, your majesty, for the Lord has saved me. The lions did me no harm because I have done no wrong.'

The king was overjoyed to find Daniel alive and unharmed. 'Take him out of there immediately,' he ordered the guards.

When the king remembered how

he had been tricked into making this law, he had the servants who plotted against Daniel arrested and thrown into the den of lions in his place. Then Daniel was put in an even more honoured position than before. In addition, he made it law that everyone in Babylon should serve and worship the God to whom Daniel prayed, and who had saved him from the lions.

he Israelites return to the Promised Land

The people of Israel remained in exile in Babylon for many more years. They were ruled by the kings of the country and, although they longed to return home, they were not allowed to do so.

These years of captivity in a foreign country were the result of the disobedience of the Israelites. They had forgotten the Lord who had taken their forefathers out of Egypt long ago, and had led them to the Promised Land. They had also worshipped false gods. Instead of becoming a prosperous, happy nation in Canaan, they were a scattered and sad people.

Finally their punishment came to an end and the Lord allowed them to return to their own land. They set out, a great parade of happy people and, after a very long journey came at last to Canaan. But they were dismayed when they reached their homeland, for all their houses had been burned and the wall around Jerusalem had been broken to pieces. The beautiful temple of Solomon had been burnt to the ground, and nothing was left except a pile of stones.

The people immediately started to work, building houses and rebuilding the temple. They began to repair the city walls and after many years of hard work, and with great difficulty at times, the task was completed. Finally everyone returned from exile to their country and to their new homes.

The people of Israel no longer prayed to idols, for they didn't want to forget God again. They prayed only to the Lord and brought offerings to him in the new temple. They also began to read the books written by the prophets about the history of their people, and about the laws which they must obey.

THE NEW
TESTAMENT

The man who received the Good News

A man and his wife called Zechariah and Elizabeth lived in a house in the mountains of Israel. Zechariah was a priest, whose duty was to tell the people of Israel about the Lord, pray for them and bring offerings to God on their behalf.

Zechariah and Elizabeth were good people who loved the Lord very dearly. They had no children. Years before, while they were still young, they had often prayed for a child but it seemed as though the Lord had not been listening to them. Now they were old and no longer believed that it would be possible for them to have a child, so they had stopped praying about it.

One day Zechariah had to make a trip to the Temple in Jerusalem. He put on his best clothes, his beautiful white priest's robes and set off on his journey. It was a long way to Jerusalem from where he lived, but he finally reached the city and made his way to the Temple of the Lord. Many other people were making their way there to worship and pray and to bring offerings to God.

In front of the Temple was a large open square where the people bought their offerings. They could buy sheep or doves and then give them to the priests, who would kill them and lay them on the fire, which had been built specially for the purpose. The meat would burn and the smoke would rise to heaven as a sign to God which meant, 'Lord, we love you and we want to give you a gift.'

Another offering was made in the Temple, but not everyone could go inside. In fact only one priest could go in and, since all the priests wanted to give the offerings, they drew lots to see who would be the chosen one. On that particular day, Zechariah was the priest chosen to make the offering.

While everyone else waited outside, Zechariah went into the Temple very reverently. He entered a large room with walls of gold, where seven golden lamps burned. The light from the lamps shone on the walls and it was very quiet. Zechariah was all alone in the Temple of God.

Standing in the golden room with the seven lamps was a golden bowl with little coals of fire in it. Zechariah had to present the offering, so he sprinkled little grains of incense on top of the burning coals. This gave off a sweet smell and was called the incense offering. While Zechariah was busy with the ceremony, he prayed silently for the people waiting outside.

Suddenly he stopped praying! He was startled, because he felt that he was no longer alone. Beside him stood a man in white robes just like those Zechariah was wearing. He wasn't a priest, but an angel who had come to give him a message from the Lord! Zechariah was very afraid and he trembled, but the angel said, 'Don't be afraid, Zechariah, for I have come to bring you good news. Your prayers have been heard and your wife Elizabeth will have a son. You must name him John.'

Zechariah didn't understand how this could be, for he and his wife were both quite old now. He just stood there shaking his head in disbelief. 'The child will make you very happy,' said the angel, 'and many others will be glad also, for he will be a servant of God. When he is grown, he will tell all the people that the Saviour is coming soon.'

This news should have made Zechariah happy, for the people of Israel had waited a long time for the coming of the Saviour, but the old man couldn't believe it! 'No,' he said. 'This can't be so. I'm old and Elizabeth is old, how can I believe such a thing? What you say would be a miracle!'

'I am Gabriel and I live with the Lord in heaven. God himself has sent me to give you this news. Don't you believe the Lord anymore? I will show you that the Lord can work miracles, and I will also punish you for not believing me. You will be unable to speak a word until all the things I have told you have happened.'

With that, the angel disappeared and Zechariah found himself alone once more in the Temple. Outside in the outer court the people stood waiting for the priest to return with the words of blessing. When he did appear, however, he said nothing. He opened his mouth to utter the words of blessing from the Lord but no words came out.

'What has happened to him?' wondered the people. 'What has he seen in the temple that he cannot speak?'

But Zechariah could not explain what had happened. When he had finished all he had to do in the Temple, he made his way back home, anxious to give his wife the good news that God had answered their prayers. There was no more doubt in his mind about what the angel had told him and he wanted to sing for joy - but couldn't!

As soon as he arrived home, he took a little piece of slate on which to write and told Elizabeth everything that had happened in the Temple. 'His name will be John,' he added at the end.

Less than a year later Zechariah and Elizabeth had a baby boy. When all the neighbours and friends heard about it they were very pleased for the couple, whom they knew longed so much to have a child. When the baby was eight days old they came to visit the priest's home to join in the celebration, for on this day the child would be given his name.

They thought, of course, that the baby would be called Zechariah after his father as was the custom, but Elizabeth told them his name would be John. 'John?' they asked, surprised. 'What a strange name! We will ask Zechariah if this is to be his name.'

'What will the baby's name be?' they asked Zechariah.

Zechariah still couldn't talk, even though he wanted to tell them, so he took his writing slate and wrote, 'His name will be John.'

Suddenly Zechariah was able to speak again; everything that the angel had said had come true 'Yes,' shouted Zechariah. 'John is his name, for the Lord has heard our prayer!' Then he sang for joy, singing a lovely song in honour of God.

'How amazing everything is about this child,' thought the people. 'This is no ordinary baby!' Everywhere they went they told others about Zechariah and Elizabeth and the little boy whose name was John.

he angel comes to Mary

A girl called Mary lived in the village of Nazareth, not far from Jerusalem. Although she lived in an ordinary house, she was in fact, a descendant of King David, the great king who ruled Israel many years before.

Nearby lived a young man called Joseph, a carpenter, and he too was a descendant of King David. Mary and Joseph were very much in love and wanted to get married. Although they were both of royal descent they were poor, and would live in an ordinary house after their wedding, not in a palace.

These were hard and cruel times for the people of Israel. But everyone hoped for happier days because the Lord had promised that a child would be born who would grow up to be King and set the people free.

One day Mary was in her house alone when she hear a voice speaking to her. 'Mary, you are the most favoured woman in all the world!' When Mary looked up she saw an angel. It was the angel Gabriel and he wore a bright white robe.

'Don't be afraid, Mary,' he said. 'I am going to tell you something wonderful. The Lord has sent me to you. In a little while you will have a baby son and you will name him Jesus. When the baby is grown he will be King.'

When Mary heard this her heart sang, for then she understood. The child would be the Saviour who would come to save his people and she was to be his mother.

'Who will be the father of the child?' asked Mary. 'I am not yet married.'

'God will be the father,' answered the angel. 'This is why he will not be an ordinary child. He will be a holy child and he will be called the Son of God!'

Mary bowed her head and said, 'Then everything is well. May it all happen just as you have said.'

The angel Gabriel had done his work so he returned to heaven. He had brought the most wonderful message ever to be given to the world.

he baby in the manger

Mary and Joseph married as they had planned. God had also spoken to Joseph to tell him the news about Mary and the special baby that would be born to her.

One day they had to travel to Bethlehem, the city where King David had lived long ago. They had been told to go there by the Roman emperor, who wanted to do a count of all the people living in the empire at the time. Everyone had to return to the place where they had been born and write down their names and other details about their life.

It was a long tiring journey to Bethlehem for Mary and Joseph. By the time they reached the outskirts of the little town, Mary in particular was exhausted as she was was expecting her baby soon. It was evening and the sun had almost gone down.

'It's only a little further, Mary,' said Joseph. 'We're almost there, and soon we can find ourselves a little place where we can sleep tonight.'

Together they walked into Bethlehem, but it was almost dark when they came to a big house, an inn, where travellers could rest and have a room for the night.

However, many people were travelling at that time and they all had to have a place to sleep. The inn was full. Joseph

CENSUS — The special name given to the official head count of all the people in the land. This was carried out at the command of the Roman emperor.

CENSUS — A census took place to check that everyone was paying their taxes and taking their turn to serve in the army.

didn't want Mary sleeping outdoors that night with the baby due anytime. Nearby was a stable which would at least give them shelter and there was straw for them to make a bed to lie on.

That night, the baby that the angel had promised was born in the stable in Bethlehem. Mary and Joseph were very happy. Mary didn't have any special clothes for her baby but she took some pieces of cloth and wrapped him up to·keep him warm. They had no crib either, but Joseph took a manger used for feeding the animals and made a little bed of straw in it for Mary to lay the baby.

'He will be called Jesus,' said Mary. 'This is what the angel said.'

T he shepherds of Bethlehem

In the middle of the night in which the Saviour was born, there were some shepherds in the fields of Bethlehem. The people in the town were sleeping but the shepherds remained awake to guard their sheep. They had built a fire and were sitting around it with the sheep sleeping close to them. The stars twinkled over their heads and the wind rustled gently in the grass. All was calm and still.

Suddenly the shepherds were startled, for it seemed as though the sun had begun to shine. In the middle of a very bright light stood an angel who had come from heaven. The shepherds were terrified and hid their eyes.

'Don't be afraid,' said the angel, 'for I have come to tell you something which will make you glad. Tonight the Saviour who is Christ the Lord has been born in Bethlehem. You will find the baby wrapped in soft clothes and lying in a manger.'

Then the sky was filled with a huge choir of angels singing: 'Glory to God in the highest, and peace on earth to all men.'

As the angels sang they soared higher and higher back to heaven. Then all was quiet once again in the fields of Bethlehem. The shepherds, however, didn't

go back and sit by their campfire. 'Let's go to Bethlehem, where we can see what the angel has told us about. The Saviour has been born!'

When they came to Bethlehem they found the stable and when they went in, they saw two people just like themselves. They told Mary and Joseph what had happened to them in the field while they were looking after the sheep.

Then they saw the baby, an ordinary baby, just like any other they had seen before, but they knew that this was the Saviour. He lay in the manger, wrapped in soft pieces of cloth, just as the angel had said. This was the Saviour who had come to his people. The shepherds then knelt down in front of the manger to worship him.

Shepherds had an important job
looking after their sheep.
They had to -
- find water and grass for the sheep to
  eat
- protect the animals from the weather
- protect the sheep from any fierce
  creature
- search for any sheep which had
  strayed and bring them back

SHEPHERDS

Jesus likened
himself to a
shepherd.
He called himself
the
Good Shepherd

T he baby in the Temple

Joseph and Mary took the baby with them to Jerusalem, to the Temple. They wanted to tell the Lord how happy they were with the baby and to ask Him to bless and care for the little child.

Had they been rich, they would have bought a lamb in the outer court but they were poor, so they would have to buy two doves instead. When they arrived in Jerusalem, Mary carried Jesus through the streets. Many people were walking about, but no one paid any attention to the little baby in Mary's arms. No one knew that he was the Saviour for whom they had waited so long.

At the Temple, Joseph bought the two doves and gave them to the priest, who held his hands above the child and said, 'The Lord bless you...' Suddenly an old man came walking straight towards Mary. Tears rolled down his cheeks because he was so happy to see the child in her arms. His name was Simeon, and he knew who the little child was, because God had told him.

Simeon had longed for the coming of the Saviour and had often been sad because it had seemed such a long time to wait. But God had told him, 'Don't be sad, for before you die, you will see the Saviour.'

Now the child was here, the one for whom Simeon had waited so long. He was so happy, he took Jesus in his arms and said, 'Now I am ready to die, Lord, for I am at peace. My own eyes have seen the Saviour!' Then he sang for joy just as the shepherds had done after they had seen the baby Jesus!

The Two Doves

Joseph took his family to the Temple to fulfil the Law of Moses. Some people offered a lamb as a sacrifice, but poorer people gave pigeons or doves.

Names

Anna is another version of the name Hannah, and means 'gracious'. In the Old Testament Hannah praised God for Samuel. In the New Testament Anna praised God for Jesus.

Then a litle old woman came shuffling along. Her name was Anna and she knew about the Saviour too. As she looked down on Jesus, she cried, 'This is the Saviour! How happy I am for he has come at last!' Anna then hurried down the street to tell everyone that she had seen the Saviour.

After visiting the Temple, Mary and Joseph returned home with Jesus, full of joy for all that had happened that day.

The Wise Men from the East

One night wise men from the East were gazing heavenwards studying the stars, when they noticed that a new one had appeared. It was a big star and it shone brighter in the sky than all the others. They stood gazing at it in wonder. 'A new star,' they said. 'That must mean that a child has been born somewhere and it is such a beautiful star it must mean the child is very wealthy and important. It must be the child of a king!'

For a long time they watched the star and talked about this royal child. Then one of them said, 'We must try to find this king so that we can kneel before him for surely there has never been so rich and mighty a king on this earth before.'

So the wise men set off to look for the newborn child. Their servants went to fetch the camels and the wise men prepared beautiful expensive gifts. They even took a chest of gold. Then they mounted their camels and began to journey in the direction of the star.

It was a long journey over high mountains and through great forests. They had to ride through countries that they had never visited before, until they reached Israel. The young king for whom they were looking must be in this land, but how could they find him? They travelled to Jerusalem, the largest city, and on to the palace, where surely a king would have been born.

They requested an audience with King Herod, the cruel leader put there by the Romans. When he heard their story he became alarmed. How was it that the wise men were looking for the king of the Jews? 'I am the king!' thought Herod. 'And I want to remain king. Could there possibly be another king, a young king who has just been born? This cannot be, for I want to reign alone! I must know where I can find him and then I had better kill him for this child must never become king.'

Herod called on the scribes, who knew all about the sacred writings, to find out from the prophecies where this king would be born. 'It is written that he will be born in Bethlehem,' they told him.

Then the king spoke to the wise men. He asked, 'When did you see this beautiful star?'

'It was a long time ago,' they replied. 'We first saw it when we were still in our own country and we have been looking for the young king ever since but without success so far.'

'Then I will help you,' said king Herod. 'He is in Bethlehem. Go there quickly and look. When you have found him, come and tell me, for I also want to go and kneel before him.'

The wise men didn't know that the king was wicked, and they quickly went on their way to Bethlehem, following the star as they had done before. It led them to Bethlehem where it seemed to stop above a little house.

They got off their camels, opened the door and went inside, where they found Mary and Joseph and the child Jesus. He looked like any other child and they wondered if this was indeed the one they had been looking for. When they spoke to Mary and Joseph they knew that they had come to the right place. He was no ordinary child but was the one who would be the Saviour of the world.

The wise men knelt before the young king to worship him and gave the presents of gold, sweet smelling incense and myrrh. These were expensive gifts to bring but they gave them gladly, for they were pleased to have found the one they had been looking for.

When they slept that night in Bethlehem, God spoke to them in a dream. He told them not to return to Jerusalem to King Herod, who wanted to kill the child, but to return home another way. So the wise men set off back to their own country. Their journey had been long and interesting and one that they would never forget.

King Herod

In the meantime, Herod was wondering why the wise men had not returned to Jerusalem to tell him where the child was in Bethlehem. He was eager to find the baby in order to make sure he would never become king. But God had plans to protect Jesus.

Joseph had a dream in which an angel spoke to him: 'Take the child and his mother and go away from here quickly. Go to Egypt and stay there until I tell you it is safe for you to return.' Joseph woke up and told Mary what the angel had said. They immediately set off on the long journey to Egypt, where they would be safe from Herod.

King Herod was unaware that the baby had escaped as he waited for the wise men to return. Finally his patience ran out when he realised that they were not coming back.

That night he ordered that all baby boys in Bethlehem should be put to death. 'Now there is no chance that the king will still live to take my place,' thought Herod.

After Herod died, an angel told Mary and Joseph that it was safe for them to return to Israel. They made their way back, not to Bethlehem, but to Nazareth where Joseph worked as a carpenter.

Several people in the Bible had dreams in which God or angels spoke to them. Often they were warned about something that was going to happen.

DREAMS

Some of those people were:
Joseph, Daniel, Jacob, Pharaoh,
King Nebuchadnezzar, Solomon

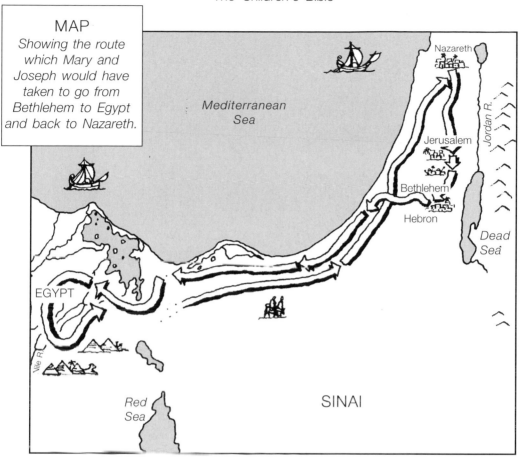

MAP
*Showing the route
which Mary and
Joseph would have
taken to go from
Bethlehem to Egypt
and back to Nazareth.*

J esus as a boy

When Jesus was a boy he lived in Nazareth with Mary and Joseph. He looked like any other boy but Mary knew in her heart that he was different, for he was the Son of God.

Every year Mary and Joseph travelled to Jerusalem to celebrate the Feast of the Passover.

When Jesus was very small he probably stayed at home but, like all Jewish boys, at the age of twelve, he was allowed to go to the feast for the first time.

THE PASSOVER

The Passover was the special meal shared by Hebrew families immediately before God rescued them from slavery in Egypt.

The angel of God 'passed over' the Hebrew houses when he saw the blood of the lamb, but struck down the firstborn in each Egyptian family.

The Passover festival is still celebrated today by the Jews as a reminder of God's faithfulness to his people.

The family travelled together that year to the Temple where the feast was held, to bring their offering and pray to the Lord.

The feast lasted for seven days and then everyone would return home. When Mary and Joseph got ready to make the journey back they could not find Jesus anywhere.

They didn't worry at first as he was always sensible and obedient. They thought perhaps he had gone ahead with the other children and they would soon catch up with him on the road.

They kept a look out for him as they made their way but were concerned when they did not see him. When evening came and there was still no sign of Jesus, they decided to turn back to Jerusalem to look for him.

They searched for three days and finally looked for him in the Temple, which was quiet now that the crowds had gone home.

As Mary looked around she was relieved to see Jesus sitting among the wise old men, listening to what they had to say and asking questions.

Never before had they come across a boy who understood them so well and could give such good answers.

Mary ran towards him. 'Jesus,' she said, 'why did you do this to us? Your father and I have been so worried! We have been looking everywhere for you!'

'Why did you look for me?' asked Jesus. 'Didn't you know I must be about my father's business?' Then Mary knew that Jesus hadn't been disobedient. She had worried about him because she had forgotten for a moment all that she knew. They then returned home as a family to Nazareth, where Jesus lived until he grew up.

J ohn the Baptist

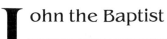

John, the son born to Zechariah and Elizabeth in their old age, grew up to become a servant of God. When he left home to start his ministry he lived in the desert, where God spoke to him and told him what he should do.

People from all over would go out to hear him preach. 'Repent, turn from your sin and be baptised,' he would say, 'for the Saviour is coming very soon.'

To teach the people that God wanted to give them a clean heart he would take them to the river Jordan to be baptised.

When people heard John preaching, they asked, 'Is this the Saviour, the Messiah for whom we are waiting?'

But John told them that he was not the Messiah but only his servant. 'No, I am not the Saviour. He is greater than I am and I am not worthy even to tie his shoelaces!'

When John was preaching one day, Jesus came by, and John was pleased to see him.

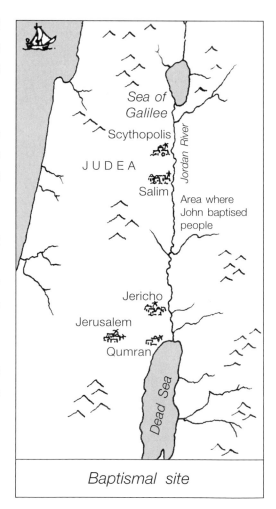

Baptismal site

PERSONAL PROFILE

NAME: John the Baptist

PARENTS: Elizabeth and Zechariah

PLACE OF BIRTH: Judea

OTHER PLACES OF RESIDENCE:

The Desert

POINTS OF INTEREST:

His clothing was made of camel hair

He ate locusts and wild honey

He preached about Jesus' coming

He baptised Jesus in the Jordan river

The angel told Zechariah that John

was not to drink wine or strong drink.

The name John means, *the Lord is*

gracious.

JOHN THE BAPTIST & KING HEROD

King Herod had John arrested, bound and put into prison. He did this because John spoke out about some of the wrong things Herod was doing. However, he liked to listen to John speak and was afraid to kill him.

During a special feast, to celebrate the king's birthday, Herod had John beheaded in order to keep a promise he had made to his daughter.

When John's disciples heard that he was dead they took his body and placed it in a tomb.

John was surprised, however, when Jesus asked him to baptise him. Why should someone who was without sin wish to be baptised like other people?

When he questioned Jesus, he insisted that John should do it, so they walked into the water together.

When Jesus came out of the water, a voice came from heaven which said,

'This is my Son, whom I love.'

Then what looked like a white dove came down from the sky and rested on Jesus' head.

The dove was a symbol of the Holy Spirit and John knew without doubt that this was indeed the Lord Jesus, the Saviour of the world.

After Jesus had left to start his ministry, John called to the people, 'Repent, for the kingdom of heaven has come!'

Soon John's work would be over, and the Lord Jesus would tell others about the kingdom of God.

he first disciples

Jesus was walking along beside the sea when he saw a fishing boat close to the shore. There were two brothers in it, one called Peter and the other Andrew. He stopped to watch the two men working and shouted to them, 'Come and follow me and I will make you fishers of men.' Andrew and Peter did as they were asked, leaving their fishing boat and their nets to follow Jesus and become one of his disciples.

A little further along there was another boat which had been pulled up on to the shore while the men mended their nets.

There was an older man and his two sons, James and John. Jesus called the two sons to also leave their nets and follow him.

Later others joined the group until Jesus had twelve disciples. They followed Jesus everywhere and were pleased to become his friends.

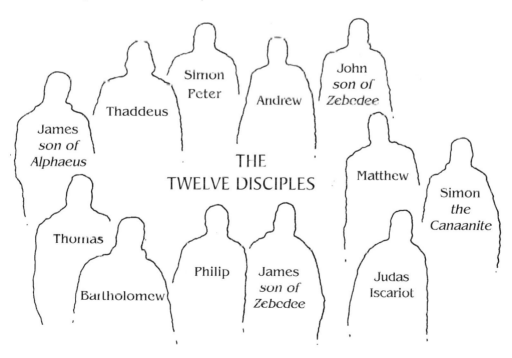

Water into wine

Jesus was once invited to a wedding along with his mother Mary and some of his disciples. It was a happy occasion, with music, delicious food and good wine to drink.

However, in the middle of the feast, the wine ran out, but only a few people were aware of it. Mary got to know about it and told Jesus, who spoke to the servants. He asked them to fill six large jugs with water then pour some out for the guests.

The servants did as they were told and when they poured it they were surprised to see that wine flowed out. 'Surely this is no ordinary man,' they said to each other as they took the wine to the guests.

The guests knew nothing about what had happened but commented to their host, 'Most people offer the best wine first, but you have saved it for the last!'

J esus reaches out to others

The Lord Jesus travelled widely with his disciples, preaching and healing the sick.

Many who were blind came to him; along with others who could not walk or who had diseases which could not be cured. He welcomed everyone who came to him.

There were also those who came to share their worries with him and to ask him how they could have eternal life. Then he would pray with them and tell them that he had come to earth to forgive their sins and bless them. But first they had to turn from their sins and trust in him.

They came from far and near in their hundreds, and sometimes in their thousands, to hear what he had to say.

Although the crowds often flocked to meet him, Jesus always had a special place in his life for the disciples and liked to spend time with them alone.

Once, when they came near to the seashore where Jesus first called the fishermen to follow him and become his disciples, Peter and Andrew decided to leave the rest for a while and go out fishing in their boat. They fished all night but caught nothing, so they returned to the shore and began to rinse out their nets.

As they were busy doing this, Jesus came along, followed by a large crowd, and he stopped at the water's edge to speak to them.

AMAZING MIRACLES

Jesus carried out several miracles which involved fish.

Twice Jesus told fishermen to cast their nets into the water when they had fished and caught nothing. After obeying his instructions they received an enormous catch of fish. The quantity was so vast it almost broke their nets.

Jesus fed the crowd of 5,000 and the 4,000 using fish and also bread.

On one occasion, a coin was found inside a fish's mouth.

Everyone wanted to get near to him so they pushed and jostled until Jesus was nearly in the water. He then asked Peter to get his boat and push it out into the water so that he could stand in it just off shore and continue to speak to the gathering of people.

As the sun got hotter towards noon, Jesus stopped preaching and the crowds dispersed. 'Let us go out a little further in the boat,' Jesus suggested to Peter, 'and try and catch some fish.'

'But master, we have fished all night already and caught nothing,' said Peter, who knew very well that mid-day was not the best time to go fishing.

Nevertheless, he did as Jesus said, sailed further out to sea and cast the nets overboard.

FISHING FACTS

Many men found work as fishermen around the Sea of Galilee. They either bought their own boats or they were hired to work on someone else's boat.

The fish shape is used as a symbol for Christianity. The Greek word for fish is Icthus. The letters in the Greek language stood for: Jesus Christ, Son of God, Saviour.

Jesus likened the job of catching people to follow him to fishermen - they became fishers of men.

The most common way to cook fish was to broil it - a type of cooking that is often done over a fire, like grilling.

After a short time, when they tried to pull in the nets, they were so heavy with fish that they could not move them. They saw James and John in another boat and called them over to give them a hand. Together they were able to bring the catch on board. In fact they were able to completely fill both boats.

Peter was so surprised that he knelt before Jesus and asked him to forgive him for doubting.

T he man with leprosy

There was once a man who had leprosy; he had ugly sores all over his body. People were afraid to go near him in case they caught the disease themselves, so the poor man was forced to live in a little shelter outside the city. His friends would bring him food and place it at the entrance to his hut before running away. When he did venture into the city people would shout, 'Leper! Leper!' or he himself would cry out, 'Unclean! Unclean!' He lived a very sad and lonely life.

One day Jesus came near the city. The man had heard about him before and knew that he had healed the sick in other places so he decided to look for him.

As he made his way along the streets, people began to avoid him as they shouted, 'Leper! Leper!' He wondered if he would ever manage to find Jesus. Then he saw the Lord surrounded by a crowd of people all wishing to speak to him or have him touch them so that they too might be healed.

MEDICINAL REMEDIES

These are some of the items which were used as medicines in Bible Times:

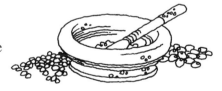

* *Parts of trees or plants*

* *Herbs, minerals*

* *Fruit, berries*

* *Wine*

* *Salt*

* *Oil*

* *Ointments, salves*

* *Potions*

- Some of these items may have been taken, if suitable, or placed on the skin.

- Cloths may have had one of these items rubbed into them. The cloth would then be heated and placed on the infected area.

- A bath containing some of these ointments may have been taken.

When the leper approached, they began to shout at him to go away. But as he came close to Jesus he stretched out his hands saying, 'Lord, will you please make me well again. You can do it, if it is your will.'

Jesus did not chase the man away for he was not afraid of his sores. Instead, he touched the leper, placed his hands on his head and said, 'Of course I will. You are clean.' Immediately the sores were healed.

The man thanked Jesus, praised God for healing him and went on his way rejoicing. Now that he was strong and healthy again he was able to return to his own home and his family.

he man who couldn't walk

The Lord Jesus was inside a house speaking to a crowd of people. Every room was crammed full and they jostled to get as near to him as possible. There were four men who were particularly keen to get close to Jesus.

They had a friend who was crippled and they had to carry him on a mat. The man believed that God was angry with him and that this disease was some kind of punishment for his sins.

OTHER HEALING MIRACLES

Jesus healed many people.

Some of the problems which he cured were:
* *Leprosy*
* *Lameness*
* *Blindness*
* *Dumbness*
* *Fevers*
* *Demon-possession*
* *Deformed limbs*

Some of the people he cured were:
* *Simon Peter's mother-in-law*
* *Blind Bartimaeus*
* *Malchus*
* *Lazarus*
* *Jairus's daughter*
* *The centurion's servant*

BUILDING REPORT

Area of Interest:
Flat Roof

Materials:
Tiles made from clay

Access:
*Stairway from ground level built
on the side of the house*

Uses:
*Suitable place to do
various household tasks,
such as meal preparation
or cloth-making,
also used for sleeping*

Reasons for Usage:
*Houses often had only
one window, therefore an
open area was useful*

However, with the crowd of people in the house that day it seemed impossible for the men to get near enough to Jesus to speak to Him.

Then they had an idea. Outside there was a stair which led to the flat roof of the house. If only they could take their friend up there, they could make a hole in the roof and lower the man down to where Jesus was standing inside.

And that is what they did. They tied rope to each corner of the mat and carefully placed the man in front of Jesus while he was talking.

Jesus looked at the man and knew what he wanted without asking him. 'Don't be afraid,' he said, 'your sins are forgiven. Now, take up your bed and walk.'

Immediately the man did what he was told and he leapt up, praising and thanking God for such a miracle.

The people in the room could hardly believe their eyes. 'We have never seen anything like this before. How good and mighty the Lord is.'

Jesus raises a man from the dead

Jesus and the disciples were visiting a city called Nain. As they approached the city walls a funeral procession was coming out of the gate. Among the mourners there was an old mother crying loudly. The body being carried out that day was her only son. She had already lost her husband and there would now be no one to look after her at home.

As Jesus watched the line of mourners, he felt sorry for the old woman and said to her, 'Do not cry.' As the woman dried her eyes and looked up, the Lord Jesus walked over and placed his hand on the young man's body. Then he said, 'Young man, wake up.'

The crowd were astonished when the man stirred, opened his eyes, sat up and began to talk. Then Jesus took him by the hand and led him to his mother. The woman threw her arms round her son and hugged him. She praised God and thanked Jesus as she returned home with her son.

Jesus calms the storm

Jesus and the disciples returned once more to the seashore where crowds had gathered to hear him and had brought the sick to be touched by him. As he had done before, he got into Peter's boat when the crowd crushed against him, near to the water's edge.

When evening came, the Lord was very tired but still the people kept on coming. Eventually, Jesus said to Peter, 'Let's sail across to the other shore where we can have a rest.'

Peter set sail with the other disciples and Jesus lay down at the back of the boat and fell fast asleep.

It was a quiet evening and at first the sea was beautifully calm but, when they were half way across, suddenly the weather changed. The sky turned dark and the wind began to blow, whipping up large waves which began to beat against the side of the boat.

As the storm worsened, the waves started to crash over on to the deck, and the disciples were afraid that the boat would sink.

Jesus was so tired that he slept through it all. The disciples went over to the Lord and woke him. 'Master, help us! We are drowning! Don't you care if we all drown?'

When Jesus woke up, he heard the roaring of the wind and the pounding of the waves but he was not afraid.

'Why are you afraid?' he asked. 'You know I won't let you drown.'

Then, standing up, he said to the wind and the sea, 'Be still!' Immediately all was calm.

The disciples didn't say very much after that except, 'How amazing! Even the wind and the sea obey him.'

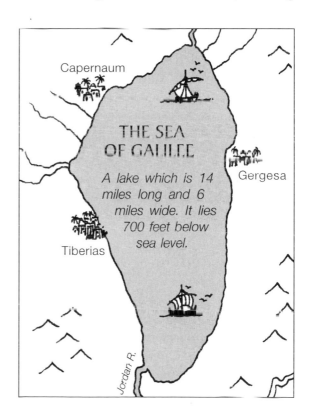

Capernaum

THE SEA OF GALILEE

A lake which is 14 miles long and 6 miles wide. It lies 700 feet below sea level.

Gergesa

Tiberias

Jordan R.

The daughter of Jairus

There once lived a man called Jairus, who was married with a daughter about twelve years old. The family lived in a house in Capernaum near the sea.

One day, however, the little girl became ill. She was so weak that she was unable to eat or drink and it seemed that she was about to die. Her father and mother were very upset.

Her father had heard that Jesus was in the area and decided to contact him to ask him to come and heal his daughter.

He ran into the street and hurried as fast as he could until he reached the seashore. There was a crowd there and in the middle Jesus stood talking to them.

Jairus pushed his way through the crowd and fell on his knees before the Lord. 'Master, please come with me right now for my daughter is so sick she may die at any moment. If you will, you can make her whole again.'

Jairus showed Jesus the way to his home, but there were so many people wanting to see Jesus that it took a long time to get there.

JAIRUS

Jairus was an official in the synagogue. He probably looked after the building and made sure that practical tasks were carried out properly.

Others stopped him on the way asking him to heal them, and that delayed him even more.

When they finally got near Jairus' house one of the servants came out to meet them, looking very sad. 'Your daughter has died. There is no need for Jesus to come to the house now, for there is nothing that can be done.

Jesus turned to Jairus and said, 'Do not be afraid, only believe that I can help her.' When they went in to the house, Jesus told all the mourners to go outside, saying, 'Why are you all crying like this? The girl is not dead. She is only sleeping.'

Then he went into the room where the girl was lying. With him were her mother and father and three of his disciples. Taking the girl by the hand he said, 'Wake up, my child.' When the girl heard the voice of Jesus she opened her eyes and Jesus gave her to her mother. 'Now, give her something to eat,' said Jesus.

T he boy who gave his lunch to Jesus

Jesus and the disciples had gone over to the other side of the Sea of Galilee where they could rest for a while, but when they crossed over in Peter's boat, they found that the crowd had gone round to meet them.

About five thousand people had gathered and, although Jesus was very tired, he didn't send them away. He continued to speak to them and heal the sick they had brought to him.

When evening came, there was nowhere for the people to go and no place for them to get anything to eat. The disciples came to Jesus and said, 'We had better send the people away so that they can go and get something to eat.'

MEAL TIMES

* *Bread was an important part of the daily diet for most people in Bible times. One of the claims which Jesus made about himself was:*
  'I am the bread of life.'

* *Cheese, fruit or vegetables, flavoured with spices or herbs, were some of the other things which people may have eaten.*

* *The normal eating routine for Jews was to have two meals a day:*
  breakfast, and an evening meal.

They were taken aback when Jesus said that they should find some food to give them. 'How can we do that? There are so many of them.'

'Go and see if anyone has any food,' said Jesus.

The disciples asked around until they found a little boy among the crowd who had brought with him five loaves of bread and two fish, but that was not nearly enough to feed the crowd.

When they told Jesus that they had only found one lad with food, he told them, 'Bring the loaves and fish to me and ask all the people to sit down.'

Jesus then took the fish and the bread and asked God's blessing on the food that had been provided.

He filled basket after basket and told them to share it out among the people.

Everyone had enough to eat that day. In fact there was so much, the disciples gathered up twelve baskets full of leftovers.

METHODS OF TRANSPORT

In Bible times the most common method of travelling was on foot. If you were fortunate enough to own a donkey or horse, these would be ridden separately or used to pull a cart or chariot.

Around the Sea of Galilee boats were used to transport people from place to place. Many of these boats would also be used for fishing and could hold approximately 12 to 14 people.

On one occasion, Jesus used a boat to preach to the crowds from the edge of the Sea of Galilee.

esus walks on the water

Jesus wanted to rest for a while so he told the disciples to go back on their own in the boat to the other side of Galilee. He would join them later. When they set out, the wind was against them and it was hard going to get across.

The sea got rough and the wind began to rise as they rowed harder and harder against the storm. Soon they became afraid and were sorry that the Lord Jesus was not with them to save them as he had done before.

Although Jesus was still on the shore resting, he was aware that they were struggling to reach the other side.

The disciples continued trying to keep the boat on course but they were frightened.

What a shock they got when suddenly they saw what looked like a ghost, a white shape looming in the darkness, walking towards them on top of the water. Then they heard the voice of Jesus, 'Do not be afraid, for it is I, the Lord.'

Peter cried out, 'Lord, is it really you? Let me come to you.'
Jesus replied, 'Why not, Peter? Come to me then.'

STORMY WEATHER

The Sea of Galilee is completely surrounded by mountains. When cool air filters through the spaces in the mountains, this causes a clash with the hot air lying over the lake. As a result fierce storms sweep across the sea, causing difficulties and rough conditions for fishermen.

Peter climbed out of the boat and stepped on to the water. As long as he kept his eyes on Jesus he was able to walk towards him, but then the wind began to blow again and the water splashed round about him and Peter became afraid. He began to sink and shouted out, 'Lord, save me!'

Jesus was already by his side and reached out his hand to pull him up. Then together they climbed over into the boat to join the other disciples and the sea became calm again.

T he man who couldn't forgive

Jesus told a story to explain why we should learn to forgive those who have done wrong to us:

There was once a king who lived in a palace with many servants. One of them owed the king a great deal of money and he demanded that he should repay him as soon as possible. But the man was unable to pay anything to him. 'Throw him in prison!' said the king to his guards.

As they were about to take him away, however, the man fell on his knees, trembling before the king saying, 'Your majesty, please have pity on me! I don't have enough money just now but I shall pay back everything as soon as I am able to. Please don't send me to prison.'

It was really an empty promise for there was no way that he would be able to repay his debts. However, the king felt sorry for him and told him that he did not need to pay anything.

The servant left feeling very pleased with himself. As he walked home that day he met another one of the king's servants, in fact a man who actually owed him some money.

He didn't owe the servant nearly as much as he himself had owed the king but he took hold of him and shouted, 'What about that money you owe me? If you don't pay up, I'll have you put in prison.'

The man shook with fear and begged him, 'Give me some time and I will repay you as soon as I have the money. Please don't put me in prison.' But the first servant wouldn't hear of it and had him thrown into jail.

PRISONS IN BIBLE TIMES

People could be imprisoned for a variety of reasons:
* *Not paying money which they owed*
* *Committing a crime*
* *For being a follower of Jesus*

SECURITY

The prisoners were well guarded and held in cells using:
* *Stocks holding the prisoners' ankles, wrists or both in place*
* *Chains*

WHO FACED PRISON?

We are told of a few believers who were put in prison because of their faith:
* *John the Baptist*
* *Peter*
* *Paul & Silas*

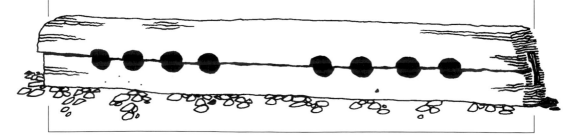

The king got to hear about the servant's actions against the man and sent for him straight away. 'You are so mean. I have forgiven you your debts so why could you not forgive the fellow servant who owed you money? For this, you can go to prison too.'

No matter how much he protested, this time the king showed him no mercy.

Jesus concluded the story saying, 'So will my Father in heaven do to you if you do not forgive the wrongs that other men do to you.'

Picture showing the seven 'I am' claims of Jesus in John's Gospel.

T he Good Shepherd

Jesus wanted to explain how much he cared for his followers and spoke about a shepherd and his sheep:

A good shepherd, he told them, knows his sheep and they know his voice. He will watch over them to make sure that they do not get into danger, leading the way to green pastures along narrow and dangerous paths, while they follow on behind.

Once they reach the good grass he will watch and make sure that none of them wander away. But if one should stray, he would call it back and bring it to the fold to rejoin the others.

He would go out into the night if necessary and search, even if only one left the safety of the flock.

Whatever the danger, from rocky ground or wild animals, he would continue looking until he had found it.

Then Jesus explained that he is the good shepherd, who looks after his flock.

If ever any of his followers wandered away from him and found themselves in danger, he would not leave them alone but search for them and care for them, bringing them back into the fold of his love.

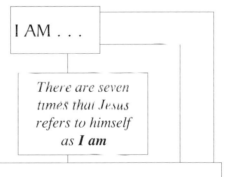

I AM . . .

*There are seven times that Jesus refers to himself as **I am***

I am the Bread of Life
I am the True Vine
I am the Light of the World
I am the Gate for the Sheep
I am the Good Shepherd
I am the Resurrection and the Life
I am the Way, the Truth and the Life

T he Good Samaritan

Jesus was speaking to a group of people one day when one of them asked, 'Who is my neighbour?' Instead of giving a straight answer, Jesus told a story to explain what he thought:

A man set off on a long journey from Jerusalem to the city of Jericho. It was a difficult and dangerous road where travellers could be attacked and robbed. The man had not gone very far when robbers hiding in the bushes set upon him. They took his clothes, beat him, stole all his money and left him for dead.

As he lay bleeding, a priest who had been to the Temple to pray passed nearby. The poor man lifted his head and asked for help. But the priest did not want to get involved so he went on his way, leaving the man by the roadside, groaning.

A little later a Levite, a servant of a priest who knows all about the law, came along the road. He was a servant of God, surely he would help. But when he saw the fellow, he did not want to get involved either, and passed by on the other side of the road.

Then a Samaritan, a man from another country, not friendly with the Jewish people, came in sight. He got off his donkey, knelt down beside the injured man and bandaged his wounds.

Once he felt that the man was able to move, he helped him up, put him on his own donkey and took him to an inn where travellers could rest and spend the night. He put him into a room and made sure that he was safe and well throughout the night.

The next morning, the man was still not fit enough to travel. The Samaritan had to get on his way, so he left some money with the innkeeper saying, 'Take

this money and look after this man until he is well. If he has to stay longer than I have paid for, let me know how much I owe you when I pass this way again.'

When he had finished the story Jesus asked, 'Which of these three men was the man's neighbour? The priest, the Levite or the Samaritan?' It was not a difficult question to answer and they replied, 'The Samaritan, of course.'

Jesus said, 'Now you must go and do the same.'

The Lost Son

Jesus told another story to his followers to explain how much God cares even for those who decide to disobey him and go their own way:

Once there was a rich man who lived in a beautiful big house. He had two sons. and they lacked nothing. The elder son was an obedient boy who worked hard every day for his father, but the younger one was lazy and did not want to stay at home to work. Nevertheless, the father loved them both equally.

One day the younger son decided that he had had enough and wanted to leave home to make his living elsewhere. So he went to his father and asked him for his share of the family money.

'I am tired of living at home,' he said, 'I want to go out and see a bit of the world before I am too old to enjoy it.'

The father was very sad that his son was not happy to stay at home with the family, and reluctantly gave him his share and let him go on his way. Every day after that he kept a watch to see if his son would come back, but the son was having a wonderful time, spending his money enjoying himself in the big city.

There he was able to buy expensive clothes, eat delicious food and go to parties. Being so rich, he had plenty of friends who were eager to help him spend his money.

It seemed as if the money would last forever and he had a great time, without a care in the world.

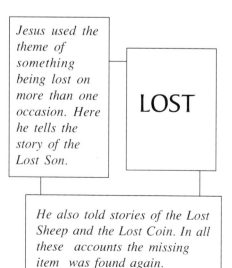

Jesus used the theme of something being lost on more than one occasion. Here he tells the story of the Lost Son.

LOST

He also told stories of the Lost Sheep and the Lost Coin. In all these accounts the missing item was found again.

192

All this time he was spending money but not earning anything to replace it. He soon found he had used up everything that he had taken with him. Then he had to start selling some of his clothes to get enough money to buy food.

When his friends realised that he had nothing to share with them, they left him. In no time at all, he did not have enough money to buy food for himself, so he had to go out into the streets and beg for a few crusts of bread. To add to his misery, there was a famine in the land and many other people were begging for food.

In despair, he asked a farmer to give him any job at all to be able to earn enough for a bit of food.

He ended up looking after pigs, and was so hungry at times that he even wished he could have the scraps of food that the pigs were eating. He felt really sorry for himself as he sat among the pigs, and remembered what he had left behind in his father's house.

He was ashamed to even consider returning home. But he got so desperate that he made up his mind that he would go back to his father, ask his forgiveness, and see if he would take him back, even if only as one of his servants.

He set off for home, and when he was still a long way from the house, his father saw him coming along the road. He had been out looking for him as he had done every day since he left home.

When he realised that it was his son struggling up the road, he ran to him, threw his arms round him and kissed him.

The son couldn't believe what was happening and said, 'Father forgive me. If you are willing to take me back I shall become one of your servants.' But his father would not hear of it, and called on his servants to clean him up and give him new clothes to wear. He even gave him a new ring for his finger and arranged to throw a party in celebration.

'Now my son has returned,' he said to everyone, 'I thought he was dead but he is alive. He was lost but now I have found him again.'

The raising of Lazarus

Jesus often visited friends in a village near Jerusalem, called Bethany. In the house where he stayed, there were two sisters and a brother, called Mary, Martha and Lazarus. They were delighted to have Jesus as their friend, and were pleased to welcome him and look after him when he was in the area.

One day, Lazarus fell ill and it looked as if he was going to die. 'If only Jesus was near,' said his sisters, 'He would come over and heal Lazarus.' But Jesus was away in another part of the country, so they sent someone to look for him and ask him to come.

When the man found Jesus he told him, 'Lazarus, whom you love, is sick and may die. Please come and visit him.'

But when Jesus managed to get to Bethany three days later, he arrived to be told that Lazarus had already died and had been buried four days earlier. Mary and Martha were in mourning but Martha went out to meet Jesus.

'If only you had come earlier, master, our brother would not have died.'
'Believe in me,' Jesus said, 'and your brother shall live again.'
'Yes, Lord,' replied Martha, 'I believe that you are Christ, the Son of God.'
'Go and call Mary,' Jesus said.

Then Martha went back to the house to fetch her sister who was being comforted by friends. 'Mary, the master is here and is calling for you.' Mary went out to meet Jesus and the others followed behind. She cried and fell at his feet, saying, as Martha had done, 'Lord, if only you had come earlier, Lazarus would not have died.'

Then Jesus began to cry along with her and comforted her. Then he asked, 'Where is Lazarus buried?'

The mourners led the way to the cave where he had been put to rest. 'Take the stone away,' said Jesus.

'What do you want to do Lord?' asked Mary. 'He has already been dead four days...'

But the Lord Jesus said, 'Believe in me, Mary, and you will see how great God is.'

Some men rolled the stone away from the entrance to the cave and the people stood back to watch what Jesus was going to do.

Jesus looked up to heaven and began to pray, then called out, 'Lazarus, come out!'

Suddenly they heard movement inside the cave and Lazarus came out, still bound up in the graveclothes he had been buried in.

They jumped back in surprise and Jesus told them, 'Take off these graveclothes and let him go home.'

Mary and Martha were so happy that day as they walked home with Jesus and their brother.

Those who had witnessed the great miracle then knew who Jesus was, and believed that he was indeed the Son of God.

TRADITIONS OF BURIAL

After death, bodies were prepared for burial by being washed, covered in oils and spices and wrapped in cloth like linen.

It was traditional for people to be buried in the same tomb as others of the family, if this was possible.

The most usual burial-places were caves, or tombs cut out of the rock.

L et little children come to me

One day a group of mothers were walking along a road with their children at their side. The older ones were being led by the hand and the smaller ones were being carried.

They were happy because they were on their way to see the Lord Jesus. 'We want our children to know Jesus. If they meet him, they will never forget him.' They also wanted to ask Jesus to lay his hands on the children and bless them.

When they came to Jesus he was alone with his disciples. When the disciples saw the mothers coming with their children, they stopped them and said, 'What do you want? Surely these children are too small and will not be able to understand what Jesus says. Children don't belong here, so don't bother Him.'

When the Lord saw what was happening he wasn't pleased with the disciples. He called the mothers and their children and said, 'Please come over to me.' And he said to his disciples, 'Let the children come to me. Don't keep them away, for the Kingdom of Heaven is for them too.'

The children stood beside him and he drew them close. Putting his arms around them he spoke to them and they knew that he loved them. Then Jesus laid his hands on their heads and blessed them.

CHILDREN

Children are very precious to Jesus. Several miracles in the New Testament show how Jesus touched their lives:

* *The little boy who gave his lunch to Jesus in the feeding of the 5,000*
* *Jairus's daughter who was healed*

CHILDREN

Many stories in the Old Testament show how God used children in a special way:
* *Miriam and Moses*
* *Joseph and his coat of many colours*
* *Samuel who served God in the temple*
* *David who fought Goliath*
* *Naaman's servant girl*

CHILDREN

B lind Bartimaeus

A man was once sitting by the side of the road with his coat thrown over his shoulders. He looked as though he were asleep. Whenever he heard footsteps he would raise his head a little and listen. When they were very close he would hold out his hand and say, 'Please give me some money so that I can buy bread!'

Although he could hear footsteps he couldn't see the people. He could hear the swaying of the branches but he couldn't see the trees. Sometimes he would smell the sweet freshness of the flowers but he couldn't see their beautiful colours. All he knew was darkness. He had to feel his way from place to place, unable to see his way. There was no work for him to earn money, so he had to live by begging from people.

The beggar's name was Bartimaeus, and he had been blind for a very long time. There was no cure for his illness. However, he had heard about the Lord Jesus and thought he might be able to heal him.

But Bartimaeus had never been near the Lord. Had he been able, he would have asked for his help, but he couldn't even look out for Jesus on the streets.

One day he was sitting by the road listening to the passing footsteps. Many people were on their way to Jerusalem for the feast of the Passover, as everyone wanted to join in the celebrations.

That particular day it seemed extra busy. There was such a large crowd that the ground shook under their feet. They were shouting and pushing each other so much that they sometimes bumped into Bartimaeus.

'Why are so many people passing all at once?' called Bartimaeus. 'What's going on?'

'Don't you know?' some of the people told him excitedly. 'Jesus is coming!'

Bartimaeus' heart began to pound in anticipation. Jesus was coming and perhaps he was close to him already. Maybe he would hear if Bartimaeus called him very loudly. So Bartimaeus began to call out, 'Jesus of Nazareth, have pity on me!'

The people nearby were very angry with him. 'Be quiet,' they said. 'Do you think the Lord Jesus has time for you? He is going to Jerusalem to be made king.'

But Bartimaeus didn't pay any attention. They didn't know what it was like to be blind and sit all day in the darkness by the side of the road. He shouted all the louder, 'Jesus of Nazareth, have pity on me!'

Then, to his delight, a voice answered, 'Bring Bartimaeus to me. He is sitting over there by the roadside and is calling me.'

Then the people shouted, 'Bartimaeus, hurry up. Come over here !'

Struggling up, Bartimaeus threw off his coat and came to the Lord. With his arms outstretched he staggered through the crowd. 'What is it you want, Bartimaeus?' said a kind voice. 'What can I do for you?'

Bartimaeus replied, 'Lord, I want so much to be able to see.'

'Since you believe that I can heal you,' said the Lord, 'now you shall see.'

All at once Bartimaeus could see again. He saw green trees and a beautiful blue sky. He saw men and women and he saw the Lord Jesus, who had healed him! Falling on his knees, he thanked the Lord for having done as he asked.

When Jesus went on his way, Bartimaeus followed behind and danced with joy. Now he was a strong happy man who would never have to beg again because Jesus had touched him.

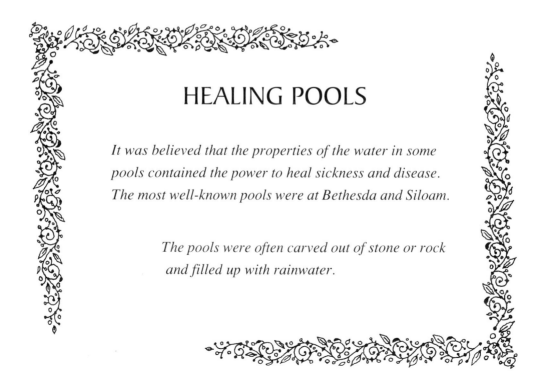

HEALING POOLS

It was believed that the properties of the water in some pools contained the power to heal sickness and disease. The most well-known pools were at Bethesda and Siloam.

The pools were often carved out of stone or rock and filled up with rainwater.

H osanna

Jesus was walking down the road which leads to Jerusalem with his disciples and other followers. They were wondering, 'Is he going to Jerusalem to become king?' This was what many of them wanted. There were enemies in the land, Romans, who treated the Jews very harshly. They believed that if the Lord Jesus were to become king, he would be able to help them defeat the Romans.

Suddenly Jesus stopped and spoke to two of the disciples, 'Do you see that village over there? You must go there, and on the outskirts you will find a young donkey tied by a rope. Untie it and bring it to me. If anyone asks what you are doing with the donkey answer, "The Lord needs it."'

The disciples wondered why the Lord would want a donkey. They thought he wanted to ride into Jerusalem. Perhaps he really did want to become king.

They walked towards the village, and there was the donkey, just as the Lord had said. It was tied near the door of one of the first houses. When they began to untie the rope, some men standing nearby asked, 'What are you going to do with the donkey?'

The disciples answered just as Jesus had told them, 'The Lord needs it.' Then the men let the donkey go.

Jesus' followers were pleased when they saw the disciples coming with the donkey. Now they knew what the Lord Jesus would do.

They took off their coats, laid them on the donkey's back and then helped the Lord to climb up. The disciples walked along booido him and the crowd followed, shouting, 'Here comes our King! Hosanna to our King!'

They pulled long palm branches from the trees and waved them like flags over his head. Some of them took off their coats and put them on the road so that the donkey could walk on them. Everyone was shouting and singing for joy. As they came closer to the city they shouted louder and louder, 'Hosanna! Hosanna!'

Watching all this were some dignified looking men standing silently in the crowd. They were the priests and the Pharisees. They didn't join in because they didn't love Jesus. They were jealous of him because the people were so fond of him. Everyone was eager to hear Jesus preach and the priests didn't like it at all. 'The people must listen to us. We are much wiser than this man!'

When they saw Jesus riding into the city, and heard what the people were singing, they became very angry. They would have pulled him from the donkey if they thought the crowd would let them get away with it.

'Hosanna, our king!' the crowd continued to shout. The angry priests and Pharisees shouted back, 'Don't say this! He certainly isn't our king!'

Then the leaders came to Jesus and said, 'Master, tell your disciples they mustn't say these things.' But the Lord Jesus said nothing, for everything the crowd was saying was true. The Lord Jesus was a king, although he was not the kind of king the people were thinking about. He was no ordinary king, not one who would lead the people against the Romans in battle, but a King of Peace.

The people didn't understand, but thought that he would become their king immediately. This was why they were so excited. But Jesus knew many things would have to happen before he would be king. Many of the things would be dreadful and difficult. This was why he was sad as he rode through the streets of Jerusalem towards the great temple.

The people crowded around him, waiting for him to say, 'Now make me your king and we will fight our enemies together.' But he said nothing as he went into the Temple that day. Jesus remained inside for a long time as the people waited outside.

ary gives a gift to Jesus

Jesus was in Bethany, where some friends lived. There was Simon, whom he had healed of leprosy, Mary, Martha and, of course, Lazarus, the man whom Jesus had raised from the dead. It was evening and Jesus was sitting at the table with them. They were about to eat and Martha was busy putting food on the table. Lazarus was sitting close to the Lord and everyone was happy because Jesus was with them again.

Just as they were ready to eat, Mary walked in, holding a very expensive jar of perfume and she looked sad. Mary knew that this would be the last time Jesus would be with them. He had told them that he would go to Jerusalem the next day and would not return. To show how much she loved him she wanted to do something special that day, so she had gone out and bought the most expensive jar of perfume she could afford. Nothing was too costly for Jesus.

The perfume was what people used in their hair, just a few drops at a time. But Mary thought a few drops weren't nearly enough. She stood behind him and let most of the precious oil run over his head. Then she knelt down and anointed his feet as well, until the sweet smell filled the house. Jesus sat quietly and let Mary do it, for he knew how much she loved him.

Most of the others, however, didn't understand why he let her do it. Judas, one of the disciples, couldn't believe his eyes and complained, 'What is that woman doing? Look how she broke that expensive jar as though it were worthless and now she is throwing away all the expensive oil! Why didn't Mary simply give the jar to the Lord just as it was, then we could have sold it and given the money to the poor.'

Although Judas was a follower of Jesus, he was not an honest man. He didn't say this because he was thinking of the poor, but probably of what he could do with the money himself.

The other disciples also complained, but Jesus said, 'Be quiet, all of you. Why are you grumbling? Mary has done what is right. There will always be poor people and you can give them something later on. Do you know why Mary has done this? I will not always be with you, because I am going to die soon. What Mary has done will never be forgotten.'

Then the disciples were quiet, for they felt ashamed of themselves. Judas however, was still upset and he got up and left the house.

J udas betrays Jesus

Judas walked alone in the darkness of the night. He was angry with Jesus. He thought Jesus was going to be king and now he had said he was going to die! How wonderful it would have been if Jesus had become king. Judas might have become one of the most important servants, with fine clothes to wear, perhaps a large house in which to live, and many other things he wanted so very much. Now he would get nothing at all.

He no longer wanted to be a disciple of Jesus. Instead, he made up his mind to go ahead with his plan to betray Jesus, even although the Lord had always been kind to him. Judas went to the enemies of the Lord, the priests and the Pharisees. 'What will you give me if I help you to arrest Jesus?' They promised him thirty pieces of silver. Judas wanted the money because he loved wealth above all other things. 'I will call you when you can catch him easily,' he said. 'I will stay with Jesus and pretend that I am still his friend.'

Stealing away into the darkness, he returned to the Lord Jesus and acted as if nothing had happened. But, unknown to him, Jesus knew all about it.

Jesus washes the disciples' feet

It was Passover in Jerusalem, and in every house tables were spread with wine, bread and meat. The feast would be celebrated in every home throughout the land. Jesus wanted to celebrate the Passover with His disciples for the last time. He called Peter and John and said, 'Go and make everything ready for the feast.'

'Which house do you want to go to?' asked the disciples.

'Go into the city. There you will see a man walking with a jug of water. Follow that man and go into the house which he enters. You must say to him, 'Where is the room where Jesus can celebrate Passover?' Then he will show you a big room with tables and chairs, all ready for the feast.'

When the two disciples went to the city they found everything just as the Lord had told them. They met a man with a jug of water and followed him into a house. When they asked, as they were instructed to do, they were shown into a big room. Peter and John prepared the supper, placing the bread, wine and meat on the table. At the entrance to the room they placed a pitcher of water and a large basin so that the disciples could wash their dusty feet.

When everything was ready, Peter and John sat down to wait for the Lord Jesus and the other disciples. It was almost evening when they arrived. When they came into the room they each looked at the basin and wondered whether a servant would come and wash their feet.

They were much too proud to wash each other's feet themselves, so they all sat down at the table with Jesus. He said, 'I want to celebrate this Passover with you as this is the last time I will be able to do it.' Then, without saying anything, he got up, poured some water into the basin, took a towel and then got down on his hands and knees in front of one of the disciples.

The disciples were shocked! Was the Lord Jesus going to do the work they had all refused to do? Was he willing to be the servant and wash their feet? They were very ashamed of themselves. Peter felt worse than all the others and when Jesus came to wash his feet he drew them away saying, 'Lord, you shall not wash my feet!'

But Jesus looked at him and answered, 'If I do not wash your feet you cannot be my disciple. You do not belong to me!' Peter wanted very much to belong to the Lord and when he heard this he had to agree. Peter loved the Lord Jesus very much so he said, 'Lord, then wash not only my feet but also my hands and my head.'

Jesus washed the feet of all the disciples, including Judas who was going to betray him. When he had finished he put the basin away and came back to sit at the table. 'Do you understand why I have done this?' He asked. 'I have given you an example, for I wanted to teach you something. You mustn't quarrel about who is the most important. You must help each other and gladly do things for one another. Don't be afraid to be a servant. You will really be my disciples if you do these things.'

The disciples felt very ashamed of themselves but they had learned a lesson. They were sorry they had been so proud. But there was one who wasn't in the least bit sorry, for he no longer really belonged to the disciples - Judas.

The Last Supper

Jesus was sitting at the table with the disciples. 'Remember, this is the last time we will be together,' he said. 'It won't be long before my enemies come to take me away and then I must die. One of you here at the table will betray me and help my enemies.'

The disciples looked surprised when he said this. Surely none of them would ever betray their master who had been with them for so long? He had always been so good and kind to them, who could possibly be so wicked as to betray him? 'Who is it?' they asked.

John was sitting right next to Jesus and he whispered, 'Lord, who is it?' And the Lord answered softly, 'The man to whom I give this piece of bread.' Then he gave the bread to Judas.

Judas also asked very boldly, 'Lord, is it I?'

'Yes, Judas!' answered the Lord Jesus. 'You are the one!'

The others didn't hear it but Judas was angry when he realised that Jesus knew all about him. 'You had better leave now and do as you have planned,' Jesus told him. He was going out to betray the Lord to his enemies.

After Judas had gone, Jesus was alone with the other disciples. They ate the bread and drank the wine, for they were celebrating the feast together. 'You must celebrate this feast, even after I am gone,' said the Lord. 'You must always keep this feast. Do you see how I am breaking this bread? My body will be broken in the same way for you. Do you see how I am pouring the wine? So will my blood be poured out for you. When you keep this feast, you must also eat bread and drink wine, for then you will remember how I died for you. You must never forget this.'

The Lord Jesus told his disciples many other things that evening as they sat together at the supper table. He told them that his enemies would come that very night to take him away. 'And all of you will leave,' he added. But the disciples shook their heads, 'No, we would never do a thing like that. We will never leave you!'

'Even if all the others leave you,' Peter protested, 'I will never leave you. I will fight for you and, if necessary, I will die for you!'

'Are you really willing to die for me, Peter?' asked the Lord. 'I tell you, this very night you will deny me three times. You will lie and say you are not my disciple at all. Before the cockerel crows tomorrow morning you will have denied me three times.'

Peter didn't believe a word of it and neither did the other disciples. But the Lord Jesus knew all that would happen that terrible night. Nevertheless, he told them not to be sad even although everything would seem to be going wrong, for all would turn out well in the end. He told them that he was going to die but that he would come back to life again. Later he would go to heaven and one day the disciples would go to be with him there.

Then they prayed together and the Lord Jesus prayed for his disciples and for all the people who would come to believe in him. When he had finished praying, he said, 'Come, let us go.' Then they went together into the darkness of the night.

The Garden of Gethsemane

Near the city of Jerusalem was a garden with many trees, called the Garden of Gethsemane.

After the Last Supper the Lord Jesus walked sadly toward the garden with the disciples. His heart was sad, for he knew it wouldn't be long before men would come to take him prisoner. They would mock him and hurt him and then kill him. It was terrible, but it had to be. Jesus had never done anything wrong and didn't deserve to be punished like this. He didn't deserve to be punished at all. The people themselves deserved to be punished for their sins, but the Lord Jesus had prayed, 'Father, I love them. Let me be punished in their place, so that those who believe may enter heaven.'

Now the time had come. The punishment would be hard and Jesus thought, 'I want to be alone. I want to pray to God to help me to bear it.'

When they reached the Garden, Jesus told his disciples, 'You had better stay here.' Peter, James and John went a little way with him into the Garden.

'I am very sad,' he told them. 'You must stay here, but don't go to sleep. Please stay awake and pray for me.' Then Jesus went a little further into the darkness of the Garden, where he fell on His knees and prayed, 'Father, I'm afraid and very sad because the time for the terrible punishment has come. I will do all that you want me to. Help me, Father, and make me strong.'

He stood up and went back to the three disciples to speak with them about his sorrow, but he found them all fast asleep. Waking them up, he said, 'Can't you stand by me for even an hour?'

But when Jesus left them again their heads sank slowly down on the grass and their eyes shut as they fell asleep again. Jesus knelt down to pray once more. So great was his pain, big drops of sweat came to his forehead. 'Father, I will bear this punishment, but please help me!'

He told God everything and said, 'Father, help me to do all you want me to do.' Then an angel came down from heaven to comfort and strengthen him.

'Let the awful punishment come,' Jesus prayed. 'I am ready to bear it.'

Suddenly the stillness of the night was broken by the sound of voices. There were lanterns swaying in the darkness and men coming into the garden. The disciples had been asleep but woke up with a start when the noise came closer. They hurried over to Jesus. Judas was leading the men and showing them where to go.

Judas told them, 'I will show you which one he is and I will behave as though I am still his friend. The man whom I kiss on the cheek is Jesus.'

When Judas and the soldiers came close to the Lord, he said, 'Hello, Master!' and kissed Jesus.

The Lord Jesus asked him, 'Judas, are you betraying me with a kiss?'

Judas didn't say anything. As he stepped back, the Lord Jesus walked over to the soldiers and asked them, 'Who are you looking for?'

'Jesus,' they replied.

'I am he,' said the Lord Jesus.

Then a very strange thing happened. All the soldiers fell to the ground as if they had been knocked over – they were shocked and surprised. Quickly they scrambled to their feet again and looked at the Lord Jesus with awe. 'Was it possible that he was so powerful as to knock us all down like that?'

'If you are looking for me do not hurt my disciples but let them go on their way,' Jesus said. Then he held out his hands to them and the soldiers grabbed him. Suddenly, Peter jumped forward, wanting to fight for the Lord. 'Let him go!' he shouted. 'Let my Master go!'

He had a sword which he swung wildly in the direction of the soldiers. He hit one of them, cutting off his ear. 'Stop it, Peter!' said the Lord 'Do not help me. The angels in heaven could also help me if I asked them, for my Father would send a thousand of them. I don't want that, however, for I must be taken.' Then he went over to the wounded soldier and healed the ear.

Jesus' enemies, however, didn't treat him so kindly but grabbed him, tied his hands tightly with rope as if he were a dangerous criminal, and led him away. The frightened disciples scattered in every direction as they ran from the Garden.

Jesus faces his enemies

In Jerusalem stood a beautiful big house. It was the house of the high priest, a man in charge of all the other priests. On the night of the betrayal of Jesus, the high priest sat with other important men.

They were all glad that Jesus had been taken prisoner and waited for him to be brought before them. 'Now we have him and we will never let him go again. He must die, for then we will be rid of him! After he is dead, the people won't be able to listen to him any more and we will once again be the leaders.'

The Lord was brought in by the soldiers, his hands bound together. The leaders looked at him angrily, but Jesus stood calmly before them. The high priest asked Jesus all kinds of questions, but he did not reply. Many came to testify against him but he had done nothing wrong. He had only spoken to people, telling them about God and he had healed the sick. The high priest and the other men knew this but they still wanted Jesus out of their way. 'Say something,' said the high priest. 'Don't you hear what people are saying about you? Have you nothing to say for yourself?'

But still he remained silent.

'Are you the Son of God?' asked the same priest.

This time Jesus answered, 'Yes, I am the Son of God. In a little while I shall go to heaven, but one day I shall come back to earth. You will all see me when I come on the clouds of heaven.'

They jumped up angrily and the high priest shouted, 'How does he dare to say these things? He is not the Son of God. He is only the son of Joseph, the carpenter. This is blasphemy! He has mocked God! What shall we do with him? How will we punish him?'

'He must die!' shouted the other men. 'Yes, he must die!'

Then they began to beat him. They spat on him and did many other terrible things to him. All the time Jesus did not complain or say a word to them.

Peter

When the soldiers took Jesus, the disciples ran away. They were afraid the soldiers would catch them too, so they hid in the darkness. Peter and John, however, quietly followed the soldiers, for they wanted to know where they were going to take the Lord.

When they saw that he was being taken to the house of the high priest, Peter didn't want to go any further. But John knew the servant girl who worked for the high priest so he knocked at the door and asked, 'May I come in with this friend of mine?' The girl let them in, and so it was that Peter got into the house where Jesus was being held.

Peter was very afraid, for he thought, 'This is dangerous. This is the house of the enemy. I hope they don't find out I'm a disciple of the Lord Jesus and arrest me too. Look how that servant girl stares at me.' Walking past the girl, he went into the inner court. Some soldiers were sitting round a blazing fire. Peter walked over to the fire to warm himself and from there he saw Jesus, standing bound in front of the priests in the next room. When the servant girl walked over to the fire, she looked at Peter and asked, 'Aren't you one of the disciples of Jesus?'

Peter was startled. 'No, not me. I don't even know the man!' Peter became even more afraid than before and walked towards the door. When he got there he found the servant girl talking with some men. When Peter came near, she said to the others, 'This man also belongs to Jesus!'

Peter was very afraid. 'No, that is not true,' he said. 'I don't know that man at all.'

Peter didn't know what to do, so he went back to the soldiers around the fire. He looked towards the Lord Jesus and saw how he was being treated. 'If they catch me,' thought Peter, 'they'll probably beat me like that too.'

All at once, one of the soldiers asked, 'Aren't you one of his disciples?'

'No!' answered Peter, swearing. Then they all looked at him and another soldier said, 'Didn't I see you with him in the garden?'

'It's a lie,' shouted Peter. 'I don't even know the man.'

All of a sudden a cockrel crowed. When Peter heard it he remembered what the Lord had said, 'Before the cockrel crows, you will have denied me three times.' Then he went outside and sobbed loudly.

'Oh Master, what wrong I have done. Dear Lord Jesus, please forgive me.'

215

ilate the Roman Ruler

The night had passed and Jesus was still with the Jewish leaders. They wanted to kill him but they couldn't do this by themselves, for they weren't the rulers of the land. The Romans were the masters of the people and the priests would have to speak to them.

The most important Roman in the land was Pilate, who was the ruler over all the Israelite people, so the high priest and the others took Jesus to him. They wanted to ask him if they might kill Jesus. Many people went with them and more joined them in the street.

Pilate lived in a fine palace and when he saw the crowd coming with the Lord Jesus, he went outdoors. 'Why do you bring this man to me?' he asked.

'Because he must die!' shouted the priests. 'He has done so much evil.'
'What did he do?' asked Pilate.

THE SANHEDRIN

The Jewish leaders were known as the Sanhedrin. They took decisions on certain legal matters but in other matters were restricted by the Roman authorities. Only the Romans had the power to sentence a person to death.

Some of the Sanhedrin had plotted to have Jesus killed. They encouraged Pilate, the Roman Governor, to find Jesus guilty.

They told him all sorts of lies, but the Lord Jesus said nothing. Pilate looked at the prisoner, standing there quietly, and saw that he didn't even seem angry with all the lies.

'This man has done no wrong,' thought Pilate. When he spoke to Jesus for a moment he felt sure that he had done nothing wrong, but he was afraid to let Jesus go because of the crowd outside. Then he had an idea.

Pilate sent his soldiers to the prison where robbers and murderers were kept and they brought a man called Barabbas to the palace to stand beside Jesus.

'As is the custom on Passover day,' said Pilate, 'one of these two men may go free and you may choose which one. Whom shall I free, Barabbas or Jesus?' Pilate was sure that they would choose a good man like Jesus rather than Barabbas, a thief and a murderer.

But he didn't know how angry the men were with Jesus. He was very surprised when they all shouted, 'Let Barabbas go!'

PASSION WEEK

The week leading up to Jesus' death is often called

Passion Week

The most notable events of the week are:

Friday:
Mary anointed Jesus' feet

Saturday/Sabbath:
Day of rest

Sunday:
Jesus rode into Jerusalem on a donkey

Monday:
Jesus put the money changers out of the Temple

Tuesday:
Jesus talked using parables

Wednesday:
Nothing mentioned

Thursday:
Last Supper

Friday:
Jesus was crucified

Pilate was shocked. 'What shall I do with Jesus?' he asked.

'Crucify him!' shouted the priests. 'He must die!'
And all the people shouted with them, 'Yes, he must die! Crucify him!'

The Lord Jesus heard it. He had done nothing wrong, but had always helped them, healed their sick and blessed their children. They had even wanted to make him their king not so long ago. Now they were angry with him and mocked him as he stood helpless, his hands tied with rope.

They shouted all the louder. 'Away with him! Crucify him, and let Barabbas go!'

Pilate then freed Barabbas because he was afraid of the people, but he tried once more to keep Jesus from the cross. Taking Jesus inside, he ordered the soldiers to pull off his clothes and they whipped him on the back. Then they threw an old robe around his shoulders and began to tease him. They made a crown of thorns and placed it on his head as they laughed at him. 'What a fine king you are.'

Jesus said nothing all this time but stood and let them do as they pleased.

Then Pilate took Jesus outside once again and placed him before the people. He was sure they would feel sorry for him, when they saw how sick and tired he looked.

But the priests had no pity and neither did the crowd. They shouted again, 'Away with him. Crucify him!'

They shouted so hard and for such a long time, that Pilate became afraid of them. 'Alright,' he said. 'Take him and do what you want with him.'

The soldiers then took Jesus away to be crucified.

G olgotha

When the soldiers led Jesus away to be crucified they took a cross and laid it on his shoulders. The cross was made of two heavy pieces of wood nailed together and Jesus had to carry it by himself to the place of execution. The soldiers walked in front of Jesus as they led him through the streets of Jerusalem. Many people went along shouting and screaming at him as they elbowed their way past each other.

The Lord had suffered a lot already and was so tired that he could hardly carry the heavy cross on his shoulders. Suddenly he fell down on the road, with the cross lying across his back.

'Get up!' shouted the soldiers. 'Pick up that cross!'

But Jesus couldn't carry it any further. Looking around, the soldiers called a farmer who just happened to come along. His name was Simon. 'Come here. Carry the cross for that man.'

The soldiers pulled the Lord Jesus along with them and Simon followed behind, carrying the cross. They left Jerusalem and came to the fields outside

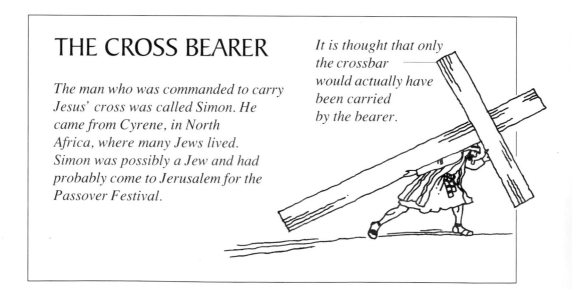

THE CROSS BEARER

The man who was commanded to carry Jesus' cross was called Simon. He came from Cyrene, in North Africa, where many Jews lived. Simon was possibly a Jew and had probably come to Jerusalem for the Passover Festival.

It is thought that only the crossbar would actually have been carried by the bearer.

the city, where there was a bare sandy hill called Golgotha. Here the soldiers drove nails through his hands and feet and then stood the cross upright in the ground.

Still the Lord wasn't angry with the men. He asked God not to punish them for their cruelty. 'Father, forgive them,' he said, ' for they do not know what they are doing.'

Two other crosses were placed next to him. On them were two criminals. The people stood and watched. With them were the priests and the Pharisees.

'Look at him,' they shouted. 'He said he was the Son of God. Why doesn't God help him now? Why doesn't he come down from the cross?'

The people mocked Jesus as he hung on that awful cross. Even the soldiers mocked him and so did one of the criminals hanging on the cross next to him. 'If you are the Son of God, why don't you save yourself and us?'

But the other criminal said, 'Be quiet. We deserve to die but this man has done nothing wrong.' Then, turning towards Jesus, he said, 'Lord, remember me when you enter your Kingdom.'

The Lord replied, 'Today you will be with me in Paradise.'

Not everyone standing near the cross was his enemy. Mary, the mother of Jesus, was there with John, one of the disciples. Mary was very sad to see how much her son had to suffer. She could do nothing and soon Jesus would be dead. Who would take care of her then?

When Jesus saw his mother, he pitied her and, looking towards John, said to her, 'Woman, behold your son.' And to John he said, 'Behold your mother.' John knew exactly what the Lord Jesus meant, so he took Mary to his home and looked after her from that time on.

The Lord Jesus hung on the cross for a long time. It was noon and the sun was high in the sky, beating down on his head. Suddenly the sun disappeared, although it wasn't evening. It grew very dark and everyone around the cross became afraid. Jesus couldn't see the sky and it seemed as though his Father in heaven wanted nothing more to do with him. It was dark for three long hours then Jesus cried out, 'My God, my God, why have you left me alone?'

Then the darkness lifted. The punishment that Jesus had to take was almost over. He cried out for something to drink. 'I am thirsty,' he groaned. Then a man came with a

long stick and on the end was a sponge. He wet the sponge and held it up to the lips of Jesus.

He cried out, 'It is finished!' then bowed his head and died. His great work was done and the way to heaven was open for all those who would trust in him.

Jesus is buried

Jesus was dead but his body was left on the cross until evening when his friends came and carefully lifted him down. They had fine linen clothes in which to wrap his body, with sweet-smelling spices tucked into the folds. Then they reverently carried him to a nearby garden where there was a cave cut into the rock. They put him inside and rolled a large stone across the entrance.

The followers of Jesus were in mourning. 'Now the Lord Jesus is dead, he can never talk to us again. He can never bless us or make us happy any more. We thought we could be happy with him, but everything went wrong!'

A BURIAL PLACE FOR JESUS

Jesus was buried in the tomb which belonged to a man called Joseph of Arimathea. He was a member of the Jewish council, the Sanhedrin.
He was a rich man.
He was a righteous man.
He was a secret disciple of Jesus.
Arimathea is situated north-west of Jerusalem.

They had completely forgotten Jesus' words, 'I shall die, but shall come back to life again. After three days I shall rise from the grave!'

Had they remembered his words, they wouldn't have been sad at all. But the enemies of the Lord Jesus hadn't forgotten his words.

The priests and the Pharisees sent soldiers to the grave and told them to watch it carefully. 'Make sure nothing happens to it,' they told the soldiers. 'The grave must stay closed and Jesus must remain inside.'

The Resurrection

It was early morning, three days after the death of Jesus.

The soldiers were still standing guard over the grave to make sure nothing would happen.

Suddenly the ground began to shake and the grave burst open. An angel in a white robe stood at the entrance and rolled the stone away. The terrified soldiers ran away as fast as they could.

At that time, the women who had helped to bury Jesus were walking towards the grave to place more sweet-smelling spices in the grave clothes.

When they came to the garden they remembered the heavy stone that had been placed at the opening of the grave and wondered, 'Who will help us roll away that big stone?'

When they looked at the grave, they were surprised to see that the stone had already been pushed aside.

One of the women, Mary Magdalene, left the others and ran back to the city to tell the disciples what had happened.

The others walked on and went inside the cave. They got a fright when they saw two angels standing over the grave clothes.

But the angels said, 'Do not be afraid. You are seeking Jesus who was crucified. He is not here, for he is risen. Come, see the place where he lay.' Then they saw that the place was empty. 'Don't you remember what the Lord told you?' they continued, 'he said, "I will die, but after three days I will rise from the grave."'

Then they remembered and were filled with joy. 'Go quickly and tell the disciples,' the angels said, 'and don't forget Peter!'

They hurried down the road when who did they meet but the Lord. He was alive and standing in front of them.

The women fell down on their knees before him, took hold of his feet and cried for joy.

Jesus said, 'Go, tell my disciples that they may also see me.'

And then the women were alone again, for Jesus was suddenly gone. But now they knew for certain that he was alive again. They had seen him and had heard his voice.

Quickly they went back to the city to look for the disciples. They laughed and shouted, 'The Lord Jesus has risen from the dead!'

But the disciples didn't believe them and shook their heads sadly. 'You must have been dreaming,' they said.

M ary Magdalene

Mary Magdalene stood near the grave, crying. She did not know that Jesus had risen from the dead, as she had run off to tell the disciples that the stone had been rolled away. While she was gone, the other women had seen Jesus. Mary still thought his body had been taken and put in another place. She was beside herself with grief as she bent down and looked inside the dark cave.

Then she saw the two men sitting there, dressed in white robes, in the place where Jesus had been. She didn't realise that they were angels.

'Woman, why are you crying?' one angel asked.

Mary sobbed, 'Because they took away my Lord and I do not know where they have laid him.' Then she turned round and saw a man standing by her. It was the Lord, but Mary could not see, for tears were blinding her eyes.

The Lord asked, 'Woman, why are you crying? Who are you looking for?'

Mary still did not see that it was the Lord, but thought it was the gardener. She cried, 'Sir, did you take him away? Please, tell me where you have laid him.'

Jesus said simply, 'Mary.' At once Mary recognised his voice.

'Master! Dear Master!' she cried. She wanted to hold him tightly and never let him go again. But the Lord said, 'Do not touch me, for I cannot always stay here. I am going to my Father in heaven again. Go and tell my disciples these things.' Then he disappeared.
Mary was no longer sad for her Master was on earth again. She ran back to the disciples and called out, 'I have seen the Lord!' and told them everything she had seen and heard. But the disciples still could not believe it.

The road to Emmaus

That same day two men were walking down the road from Jerusalem to a small town called Emmaus, where they lived. They were talking about the Lord Jesus. They said, 'What a pity it is that he died. We were sure that he would be king. We thought that he was the Saviour, the Son of God, but he couldn't have been or he wouldn't have been allowed to die.'

'And what about the stories told by the women in Jerusalem?' one asked the other. 'Can you believe them? They said that he rose from the grave but how can that be? If it is true, then he must be the Son of God. But why did he have to die in the first place?' It was all a mystery to them and they shook their heads in disbelief.

Then a man began to walk along with them. It was the Lord Jesus, but they did not realise it. He asked them, 'What are you talking about and why are you looking so sad?'

'Don't you know what has happened in Jerusalem?' they replied

'What happened?' asked the stranger.

'Don't you know what happened to the Lord Jesus?' they asked. 'You have heard about him surely. He was always good and kind. He healed the sick, gave sight to the blind and did many other miracles. But they crucified him and now he is dead. We thought he was the Saviour. He has been dead for three days, yet today we heard that there are some women in Jerusalem who say that he is alive again.'

They thought that the man would agree with them and say, 'No, that cannot be true.' But he said, 'How foolish you are. Why don't you believe it, for it is true. Jesus really has risen and now you ask why he died?'

The man told them many other things and as they listened their sadness left them. Now they understood, and were certain that he was alive.

They wanted to keep on talking to the man but, when they reached their home, they had to stop. 'Won't you stay with us? It is already evening. Soon it will be dark and you cannot travel in the night.'

The man agreed to stay and went into their house with them. He sat down with them at the table to eat. Then he prayed and, taking the bread from the table, he broke it and gave a piece to each of them.

Suddenly they recognised him. But all at once Jesus disappeared from their midst. 'We should have known,' they said, 'Didn't our hearts feel warm as we talked with him on the road?'

They hurried back to Jerusalem to tell the disciples what had happened. When they got there, they found that the disciples had locked the door, for they were afraid of the Jewish leaders. But when the two men knocked, the door was opened for them.

Before they could tell their wonderful news, the disciples called out, 'The Lord Jesus has really arisen. Peter has seen him.'

'Yes,' said the two, 'we also saw him.'

While they were still busy talking, someone else suddenly stood before them. How had he got in, for the door was locked and the windows were tightly closed? They were startled and a little afraid, but he said, 'Don't be afraid, for it is I. Come and see: touch me and look at me.'

He showed them his hands and feet with the marks of the nails still on them. He even asked them for something to eat. Then they believed that it was really the Lord. He sat with them at the table just as before and they were able to talk to him.

When he left them again no one was sad, for they knew for certain that he was alive and that he was indeed the Saviour.

At the sea-shore

Before he left, Jesus told his disciples to meet him by the sea of Galilee. Seven of them, including Peter, walked along the sea-shore watching out for him. Peter's fishing boat was tied up nearby. They waited for a while but there seemed to be no sign of the Lord. Peter suggested that they should go out fishing.

It was almost evening when they cast their nets into the water, and they fished through the night. By morning they had caught nothing. Then over the water they heard a voice calling them. A man was standing on the beach but it was still quite dark so they weren't sure who it was.

'Have you caught anything?' the man called.

'No,' they replied.

'Try casting the net on the other side of the boat,' the stranger suggested 'and you will catch fish.'

They did as they were asked and sailed further out. When they tried to pull the net out of the water they couldn't move it because it was so full of fish. The man had been right, but who could he be? John turned to Peter and said, 'It is the Lord.' Peter left the others to take the boat back to shore, jumped into the water and began to wade towards Jesus. Jesus was sitting cooking fish over a fire. By the time the rest got there, he had everything ready for them. Jesus said, 'Bring a few of the fish you have just caught.'

When Peter pulled the net up on to the beach he was amazed to find 153 fish caught in the net, which was not damaged at all. The Lord sat with his disciples in a circle round the fire. He took bread and fish and passed it to them as they talked together.

During the meal, however, Peter had many thoughts about the time he had denied the Lord before his death. Three times he had said that he was not one of his disciples. When they had finished their breakfast, the Lord Jesus said to Peter, 'Do you love me more than the other disciples?'

Peter was startled. He had once said that he loved the Lord Jesus more than the others. 'Even if all of them leave you,' he had said, 'I will never leave you. I am willing to die for you.'

Peter replied, 'Yes, Lord. You know that I love you.'

The Lord Jesus said, 'Then feed my lambs.'

For a few minutes no one said anything, then the Lord Jesus asked him again, 'Peter, do you love me?'

Peter was sad. Did the Lord Jesus not believe him? 'Lord, you know that I love you.'

The Lord said, 'Tend my sheep.'

Then the Lord Jesus asked for the third time, 'Peter, do you love me?'

Three times Peter had lied and said that he did not know the Lord Jesus. Now he was asked three times to say whether he loved the Lord. Peter sobbed it out, 'Lord, you know all things. You know also that I love you.'

The Lord Jesus replied, 'Feed my sheep. When you were young you did what you liked to do, but when you are old others will take you where you do not want to go. Follow me.'

Then Peter knew that the Lord had forgiven him and he now wished to be his servant, helping those who put their trust in him - the 'sheep' and 'lambs' that he spoke about.

esus goes to heaven

After Jesus had risen from the grave he stayed on earth with his disciples for a short time. He had finished all that he had to do on earth and it was time for him to go back to be with his Father in heaven. Before this, he met once more in Jerusalem with the disciples, except the traitor Judas, who was dead. They listened carefully to what the Lord had to say for they knew that it would be the last time they would be with him on earth.

Jesus told them that soon they would begin the work that he had taught them to do. They must go into all the world to tell men everywhere about him. It would be wonderful work but dangerous and difficult for them. He promised that through all their difficulties he would help them and care for them. 'I will not leave you alone. I will send someone to be with you: the Holy Spirit who will make you wise and strong. He will also tell you what to do, so wait in Jerusalem until he comes.'

When Jesus had told the disciples everything they should know, he walked outside the city with them to the Mount of Olives. When they reached the top he raised his hands and blessed them as he went up to heaven. The disciples remained there for a long time, gazing up to heaven. Suddenly two angels stood by them and said, 'Why are you looking up to heaven? Jesus has not gone away forever. One day he will return just as you saw him go away.'

When they heard this they went home rejoicing, and waited in Jerusalem for the coming of the Holy Spirit as he had told them to do.

he coming of the Holy Spirit

It was the Day of Pentecost, a Jewish feast, when people from all over the country flocked to Jerusalem to celebrate and worship.

The disciples gathered in a room near the Temple, waiting patiently for something to happen. Without warning there was a strange noise, like a wind

blowing among them. Some of the crowd nearby heard it too and ran over towards the house. When they got to the room they were amazed to see a group of men praying and praising God. What looked like flames seemed to be hovering above their heads but it did not burn them.

The disciples shouted for joy, for the Holy Spirit had come into their hearts just as Jesus had promised.

The people watching said, 'What is going on here? What does all this mean?' There were some who started to laugh saying, 'We know what it means. They have been drinking too much, that is why they are acting so strangely.'

Peter stood up to speak. 'No, we are not drunk. It is far too early in the day for that! What you see was foretold long ago by the prophet Joel. What you see happening was promised to us by Jesus of Nazareth, whose miracles you witnessed. He was put to death by lawless men but God raised him from the dead and he has now returned to be with his father in heaven. He has poured out the Holy Spirit on us and this is what you see and hear in this room.'

The people were greatly touched by Peter's words. 'What can we do?'

Peter said, 'You must ask God to forgive you for what you have done, believe in Jesus Christ and be baptised. Then you also will receive the gift of the Holy Spirit.'

It was certainly a Pentecost to remember that day in Jerusalem, for about three thousand people believed and came to the disciples to be baptised in the name of the Lord Jesus.

The man who was born lame

Once there was a man who used to sit near the door of the Temple and beg all day. He was born with a disease in his legs and had never been able to walk. As a result he could not work, and depended on other people to give him money to live on. When people walked past he would hold out his hand and shout, 'Please spare me some money so that I can buy bread.' Some days he was given money, but at other times nothing at all.

One afternoon the man was sitting by the Golden Gate of the Temple as usual, when Peter and John came along. When he held out his hand for some money Peter said, 'Look at us! I have no money to give you, but I can give you what I have.' Then, to the man's surprise Peter said, 'In the name of Jesus Christ of Nazareth, get up and walk.' Then he took him by the hand and helped him stand up. His feet and ankles grew strong and he was able to walk just like everyone else.

The beggar laughed and shouted with joy, leaping around and praising God. 'I can walk. I am no longer a cripple, for the Lord has healed me.' He told

everyone as he went into the Temple with Peter and John. Everyone wondered what it was all about.

'Who is that? Isn't he the crippled man who sat and begged by the Temple door?' They all came and stood around Peter and John.

Peter said to them, 'You must not look at us like that, for we did not make this man well. The Lord Jesus has done this, the same person whom you crucified. But he is not dead. He has risen from the grave and now sits with his Father in heaven.'

When the priests in the Temple heard what Peter was saying, they did not like it at all and called out the Temple guards to arrest Peter and John. The two men were thrown into prison. But many people became believers that day when they heard what Peter had to say.

The next morning the soldiers came back and brought them to the priests. 'In whose name and with what power did you heal that man?'

Peter and John then told them about Jesus and how he had sent the Holy Spirit to give them power to do things in his name. The priests could not deny that they had seen a miracle, but they were concerned that the news about

Jesus would spread. They told Peter and John, 'You must not talk about Jesus any more. If you do it again you will be punished.'

But Peter and John replied, 'God has told us to preach and that is what we must do. We shall obey him and we must speak about all the things that we have seen and heard.'

The priests were afraid of what the people might say if they punished the men who had done nothing but good. So they set them free and the two disciples went on their way rejoicing. When they joined their friends again they praised God together for what he had done for them.

eter in prison

The followers of Jesus continued to preach everywhere and many people were healed by the power of the Holy Spirit. The high priest was very angry when he heard what was happening, and the other leaders were jealous of the apostles. They wanted to put a stop to it so they had the men arrested and thrown into prison.

Peter, in particular, had caused them a lot of trouble for many years, and they wanted to silence him for good. He was sent to a secure prison before his trial and probable execution. The outer and inner doors were securely locked.

The soldiers were afraid that he might escape so he was guarded night and day by two men. There was a chain on each arm fastened to the arms of the soldiers. If he tried to get up in the middle of the night, they would waken at once. But Peter was not afraid for he trusted the Lord.

As he lay quietly sleeping in prison his friends, in a house nearby, were praying for him through the night. 'Lord, please help Peter. We cannot do anything for him now, but you can do all things.'

During the night, when the guards had dozed off, an angel came and stood close to Peter. He shook Peter awake and said, 'Get up quickly!' He stood up and as he did so, the chains dropped off his arms without disturbing the soldiers.

'Now put on your shoes and coat and follow me,' the angel continued. As he followed, the prison doors opened and they walked past the guards as if they were invisible.

Peter thought he was dreaming but realised that he was really outside when the angel led him along the street towards his friends' house. Then the angel disappeared.

PRAYER

The Bible mentions many people
who prayed in times of danger,
need or distress.

Peter's friends prayed
for his release - their prayers
were answered.

Saul prayed while blind, after his
encounter on the Damascus Road -
Ananias was sent to help him.

Paul and Silas prayed
while in prison - the Lord sent
an earthquake and
they were set free.

Jesus often prayed, and
taught the disciples
The Lord's Prayer

Paul reminds Christians to
pray at all times and to
pray for each other.

Peter knocked on the door and startled the people inside. They were still praying for him and wondered who it could be at the door in the middle of the night. Perhaps the soldiers were coming to take them to prison as well!

Rhoda, the servant girl, went to answer the door. 'Who is there?' she asked cautiously.

'Don't be afraid, open the door,' said a voice.

When she recognised Peter's voice, she was so excited that she forgot to open the door and ran back to tell the others. 'Peter is standing at the door! Peter is here again!'

'You must be mistaken,' they said.

'No, it is Peter,' said the girl. 'Listen, there he is knocking again.'

They all hurried to the door and opened it. 'Peter, is it really you? How did you get out of prison?' They all talked at once as they crowded around him.

Peter asked them to be quiet, so that he could tell them how the Lord had answered their prayers. After spending a short time with them Peter escaped, in case the soldiers were searching for him. He moved away from the area but wherever he went he continued to preach about the Lord Jesus.

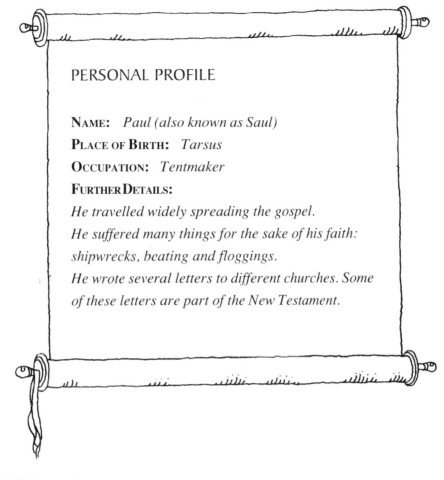

PERSONAL PROFILE

NAME: *Paul (also known as Saul)*
PLACE OF BIRTH: *Tarsus*
OCCUPATION: *Tentmaker*
FURTHER DETAILS:
He travelled widely spreading the gospel.
He suffered many things for the sake of his faith:
shipwrecks, beating and floggings.
He wrote several letters to different churches. Some
of these letters are part of the New Testament.

P aul

One of the Jewish leaders who persecuted Christians was a man
called Paul. He felt sure that it was his duty to round up those who
believed in Jesus and put them in prison. Jesus of Nazareth had
said that he was the Son of God, but Paul believed that he was an
imposter who deserved to be put to death for blasphemy.

Even after his death, his disciples were spreading lies that God had raised him
from the dead — they had to be stopped!

Paul was on his way to Damascus to arrange for the arrest of Christians and to have them brought back to Jerusalem. As he was nearing the city, a bright light suddenly flashed from heaven. He was so startled that he covered his eyes with his hands and fell to the ground. Then he heard a voice saying, 'Paul, Paul, why do you want to hurt me?'

Paul asked in a trembling voice, 'Who are you, Lord?'

The voice said, 'I am Jesus whom you want to hurt. Get up and go to the city. There I will tell you what you are to do.'

The bright light disappeared but, when Paul stood up and opened his eyes, he found to his horror that he could not see. His servants held him by the hand and took him to Damascus where they led him to a house. He sat there, still without his sight, and could neither eat nor drink. He couldn't help thinking about what had happened and he could not get that voice out of his head.

Three days later an old man called Ananias, who was a follower of Jesus, came to see him. God had spoken to him and told him to go to Paul and pray that he would get his sight back again. Ananias wasn't very sure about this because he had heard a lot about the man who had been arresting Christians. But the message from the Lord was clear, so he did what he was told.

Sure enough, when he reached the house that he had been told to visit, there was Paul. He placed his hands on Paul's head and said, 'Brother, the Lord Jesus who spoke to you on the road has sent me to you. You will be able to see again and will be filled with the Holy Spirit so that you can become one of his servants.'

Then it seemed to Paul as if dark scales fell from his eyes and he was able to see again. He stood up and said, 'Now I would like to be baptised, for I also want to be a disciple of the Lord Jesus.'

He stayed in Damascus for a few more days and began to tell others that Jesus was the Son of God. The people were very surprised and said, 'Isn't that Paul who came here to arrest the followers of Jesus and put them in prison? Now he is a disciple himself!'

The Jewish leaders were taken aback by what had happened to Paul. They were annoyed that he was now going around saying that Jesus was the Son of God. It was too dangerous to allow him to continue, so they plotted to kill him. They put spies at the gates of the city to look out for him, but he managed to escape when his friends lowered him in a basket over the wall during the night. After he escaped from Damascus he went first to Jerusalem and then to other towns and cities to preach and to meet believers. Some of the Christians didn't trust him at first, thinking that it might be a trick to arrest them and put them in prison. But when they heard what he had to say, and realised that the Jewish leaders were plotting to kill him, they knew that Paul had indeed become a disciple of the Lord Jesus.

Paul travelled everywhere to preach the gospel, not only in Israel, but to many other countries of the world.

nto all the world

Jesus had told the disciples that they had to go out into the world and preach the gospel. As they travelled around meeting people in villages and cities their work was not always easy. Frequently it was dangerous because many people opposed them, and some wanted to kill them but, with the power of the Holy Spirit in them, they were not afraid. No matter how difficult it was they continued to tell people about Jesus wherever they went.

Paul travelled furthest of all, over land and sea. Once he and his friend Silas found themselves in a city called Philippi where there were leaders who did not want to hear about the Lord Jesus. They had the two men arrested and whipped before throwing them into prison along with thieves and murderers. 'Be sure to put these men in a safe place! They say they are servants of God but they are nothing of the kind,' they told the jailor. To make sure they could not escape, the man put them into the deepest cell in the prison, chained them to blocks of wood and guarded them carefully.

Paul and Silas had every right to feel miserable in the darkness, as their backs stung from the beating and the chains rubbed against their flesh. Instead, they said to each other, 'God sees us in this dark cell and he will take care of us. The Lord Jesus suffered much for us. Now we may suffer for him.' Such was their inner strength and peace that they even sang a hymn in the middle of the night. The jailor and the other prisoners heard them, and wondered what they had to sing about.

While they were singing at the top of their voices, suddenly there was a powerful earthquake. The ground shook, the walls of the prison cracked and

burst open and the chains which shackled Paul and Silas fell off. There was nothing to stop them escaping. The jailer had fallen asleep but was wakened by the noise of the earthquake. He panicked when he stood up and realised that the walls and doors had burst open. If all the prisoners had escaped, he knew that his life was not worth living. He was about to kill himself when Paul shouted out, 'Do not harm yourself. We are all still here.'

The jailer could hardly believe his ears and rushed for a lamp. Sure enough, he found that Paul and Silas were still in the prison, although there were no chains attached to them. If they had been the evil men that the leaders said they were, why hadn't they escaped? The jailer fell down before Paul and Silas and asked them, 'Sirs, help me too! What must I do to be saved?'

Paul answered, 'Believe in the Lord Jesus Christ and you and your household will be saved.'

Paul and Silas spoke about Jesus to the jailor and he took them to his house, where he washed their wounds and gave them food and drink. Others in his house wanted to hear the message of the gospel and they too believed in the Lord. Later they were all baptised and became followers. The next morning Paul and Silas were set free by the magistrate. They went on their way again to other cities and countries throughout the world to tell people about the Lord Jesus.

For the rest of his life Paul was a faithful servant of the Lord Jesus. There were always other believers to continue the work which the first disciples had started. Many churches were set up throughout the world. The numbers grew each year as news spread about the gospel of Jesus Christ, and lives were changed by the power of the Holy Spirit.

T he story of the ten young women

When Jesus was on earth, and before he ascended to heaven, he told his disciples that one day he would return. It will be a very special day, but no one knows exactly when it will be. Certainly the whole world will be aware of it when it does come. On that day the whole world will see Jesus and know that he is the King of heaven and earth. Everyone who believes in him will celebrate his coming again.

Jesus told his followers that they should watch and pray for this special day. His kingdom will be set up on earth for all those who have put their trust in him. It will be a kingdom where there will be no crime and no wars nor arguments.

Jesus warned that there would be those who would not be happy to see that day, for they have not prepared their lives for it, nor put their trust in him to forgive them their sins. He told a story to illustrate what would happen when he comes back again:

'Once there were ten young women standing by the roadside, dressed in their finest clothes and each one carrying an oil lamp. Two of their friends were about to be married and there was to be a wedding party for them. The girls were waiting for the bridegroom to come along the road so that they could walk together to the feast. But the road was dark and quiet and there was no sign of the bridegroom, so the girls sat down and put their lamps next to them on the ground. They were tired and soon fell asleep, not realising that the oil in their lamps was nearly finished and that the lights were getting dim.

Suddenly there was the sound of music in the distance and they saw lights swaying back and forth in the darkness.

Voices shouted, 'The bridegroom is coming. Come and meet him.' But when the girls grabbed their lamps to run and meet him, they realised that they had gone out.

Five of the girls had planned ahead and had brought extra oil to top up their lamps. However, the other five did not bother to carry oil with them and wanted to borrow from their friends. 'Please give us a little oil,' they begged, 'for our lamps are almost out.' Their friends could not help them for, if they did so, they would not have enough for themselves.

So the five girls ran away as fast as they could to buy some oil while their friends led the way to the feast. They found that the room was filled with laughter and music and delicious food was on all the tables. The five wise girls sat down at the table with all the other guests and the doors were closed as the feast began.

A little later there was a knock at the door. 'Open the door please. We have now got oil for our lamps and we would like to join the feast.' The bridegroom heard them knocking and told them, 'I do not know you. You do not belong to our group of friends, for they have already come inside with us.'

So the five wise girls were allowed to celebrate the wedding supper, but the five foolish girls had to stay outside in the darkness.'

After Jesus told that story he added, 'Be watchful of your faith, for you must be ready like the girls in the story. You do not know when I will come back but you must be ready for that great day.'

S ervants of Jesus

Jesus told a story about what it meant to be one of his servants:

Once there was a rich man who lived in a big house with many servants . He was a merchant who bought and sold all kinds of things, and each year he became wealthier and wealthier. One day he had to go abroad and it would be a long time before he returned. He wanted to keep his business going during his absence so he called some of his servants to his office.

First he called in his best servant and giving him five bags of money, told him, 'Do the best you can with this money and see what you can earn for me.'

Then he called a second servant and gave him two bags of money with the same instructions. Finally, he called in a third servant and gave him one bag to see what he could make out of it. They were all told to work as hard as possible and do the best they could until he returned home.

The first servant began to work hard, buying and selling goods and making a lot of money in the process. After a while he had doubled the money and had ten bags to show for his efforts.

The second servant did the best he could but was unable to get as much business as the first. Nevertheless, he too was able to earn double what he had been given in the first place and now had four bags to return to his master.

Every day the first two servants waited for their master to return to show him what they had been able to do with his money. But the third servant did not work hard to earn money from the amount he was given. He knew very well that he could easily do something with it if he set his mind to it, but he didn't bother. In fact, he dug a hole in the ground to hide the money and then lazed around.

When the master returned he called his servants together. The first servant happily put ten bags in front of him. 'You gave me five sir, and I have earned five more for you.'

The master was pleased with him and said, 'Well done, good and faithful servant. You took good care of a few things, so now I will give you many things to care for. Go into my house and celebrate with me.'

The second servant brought in four bags of money to put in front of him. He said happily, 'Lord, you gave me two and I have two more.'

And the master was just as satisfied with him as with the first servant. He said again, 'Well done, good and faithful servant. You took good care of a little. I will give you much. Go in and celebrate with me.'

Then the third servant came. He put the one bag of money in front of his master and said boldly, 'Look, Sir, here is your money. I just put it away in the ground. I knew that you were a very hard man and I was afraid I might lose some of the money and be punished. Now you can have it all back again. I hope you are satisfied that I do not owe you anything.'

But the master was not satisfied at all. He told him, 'You lazy rascal. You knew that I was strict yet still you did nothing about it?' Then turning to one of the other servants, said, 'Take the money away from him and give it to the servant who already has ten bags. He has worked hard and deserves more, but this man has earned nothing at all.'

Jesus explained that one day he would go away to be with his Father in heaven but that he would come back again.

When he does he will ask those who say that they are his servants, 'What have you done for me?'

It may not be about what we have done with our money but in what way we have helped our neighbours.

Whatever we do for others in his name, it is as if we are doing it for him.